My passport... a saddle

by Ann Brock
née Laity

First published 2009
by Ann Brock
Chy-An-Mor, Coverack
Helston, Cornwall TR12 6SZ

ISBN 978-0-9564174-0-4
Copyright © Ann Brock 2009

Cover photo and above: 'Neapolitano', Lipizzaner stallion, Sweden 1959

Produced by Westcountry Printing & Publishing
Churchtown, Mullion, Cornwall TR12 7HQ

By the same author

Riding and Stable Safety
(David and Charles, Newton Abbott, Devon, 1980)

ISBN 0 7153 7951 8

Contents

Acknowledgments

My sincere thanks goes to…

my friend Cyril Hart, without whose encouragement and endless patience the book would never have been written.

Douglas Williams of Newlyn who made helpful suggestions, improved my grammar, and put the commas and full stops in the right places!

Rob Beadle of Lizard Computing who kindly put the final draft on computer disk.

Victor Rogers of Westcountry printing and publishing who painstakingly sorted out a jumble of photos etc. and created order out of chaos!

Finally, a special thanks to Lord Patrick Beresford who wrote such a kind foreword to this book.

Foreword

By Lord Patrick Beresford

Out of the blue an unknown caller recently identified heself as Ann Brock, saying that we had last met no less than 46 years before. At that time she was called Ann Laity, and was one of four girl grooms who had accompanied a British Team's polo ponies across the Atlantic to play in Milwaukee and Chicago. Now, whilst writing her memoirs, she politely asked whether she could quote from an article I had delivered to "Horse & Hound" about the tour all those many years ago. Of course I readily agreed, but suggested that first I should see the chapter in which it was to appear.

I had remembered Ann as an extremely capable girl who always turned herself and her charges out to perfection, and I was soon to appreciate that that excellence in the stables was fully equalled by her skill with the pen. Her vivid descriptions of people and events brought back a host of memories, so much so that I straight away requested to see the other chapters in her book.

Although it's central theme is the horse, Ann's story includes her remarkable experience on distant shores in an era when travel was far more exciting and adventurous than is now the case, particularly if undertaken on a shoestring. Consequently I feel sure that her memoirs will have enormous appeal both within and without the equestrian community. I personally found them almost impossible to put down. Her keen observation and retentive memory, combined with an enviable prose style, bring to light the colour and atmosphere of divers places in which she has spent time, from the Australian bush to the blue grass of Kentucky, from the clarity of the Great Barrier Reef to the beauty of Alaska, and perhaps the most unusual of the lot a spell under the big top of a circus in Sweden and Lapland.

All in all, a captivating tale.

October, 2009.

Introduction

It has taken me 50 years to write this story! Although I used to jot a few incidences down in a small pocket diary I had absolutely no intention of anyone else ever reading it.

However, urged on by some friends, and because I always enjoyed writing, it suddenly became a challenge and I thought "OK I'll have a go and see what happens"! As most of it has been written from memory and mine gets worse with age, I apologise for any inaccuracies!

Bosistow

Chapter 1: **Bosistow**

I remember how cold it was on that bleak November day – the day that was to change the ordinary routine of my life into one of travel and unexpected adventures.

A south westerly gale was blowing and the sea was exploding against the towering granite cliffs in magnificent fountains of pure white spray. Tiny flecks of foam, like snowflakes, floated inland and across the barren cliff top. In my mind's eye I could imagine the Land's End Hotel and just beyond it, the Longships Lighthouse, a gaunt sentinel in that cauldron of Atlantic fury.

The young horse I was riding shook his head as the salty spray stung his eyes and I felt him quicken his stride as I turned him into the wind and headed for home.

Bosistow, the farm where I had lived for the greater part of my life, is only about two and a half miles from Land's End as the crow flies and is literally one of the first and last farms in Britain. In the nearby village of Sennen there is an inn named' The First and Last'. The cliff land is a dull brown in winter but in summer it becomes beautiful with purple heather and yellow flowering gorse. It was a favourite exercising ground for horses which from early childhood had always been my chief interest. Further inland, the small fields are enclosed by low stone walls and narrow banks built of earth and rocks, which over the years have grown a thick covering of grass and wild flowers. The few gnarled trees lie askew, blasted by the south westerly gales blowing in from the Atlantic.. I was not born at Bosistow but in a tiny granite farm house called Tregiffian, a few miles further round the coast towards Lamorna Cove. There we were only a stone's throw from the sea. I can still remember the excitement whenever I saw the huge ocean liners far out to sea, creeping slowly along the horizon. At night, from my bedroom window I used to watch the flashing light of the Wolf Rock lighthouse. It would gleam suddenly and unexpectedly in the darkness; a flash of white, a few moments' pause, then a flash of red. I often wondered what lay beyond that vast expanse of heaving water. In fact, the cliff land at Tregiffian, known as Carn

2 years old. Sitting on dad's hunter 'Patch' *On 'Mistletoe' helping Dad at Tregiffian*

Barges, adjoined the potato and flower meadows described by Derek Tangye in his book 'Gull on the Roof.' The farmer from whom he rented the derelict cottage on the cliff was my dad, Harry Laity. Our much-loved Cornish poet and bard, David Prowse, writes of his childhood when roaming those cliffs in his nostalgic poem 'Carn Barges.'

During my childhood years, however, it was horses that soon became my chief interest. My earliest memory is of sitting up in front of my dad on the pommel of the saddle and being bounced up and down like a yoyo as I clung precariously to the horse's mane. On my fourth birthday I was given a pony of my own. I shall never forget Tiny. He was thirty years old; age had silvered his face and hollowed his eyes and his front legs were slightly crooked. Looking at the photo of him now, I can't think what possessed dad to enter such a tatty looking old pony in a show at Penzance. With the blissful ignorance of the very young I was completely unaware of the comic sight I must have been. I can't remember which class he could possibly have entered him in but I can remember being almost smothered by a jockey cap which fell down over my eyes and a pair of jodhpurs that would have fitted a heavyweight boxer! The judge, to his eternal credit, kept a perfectly straight face as he asked me my pony's age but when I blurted out in a voice that was loud enough for the spectators to hear, " 'ees thirty", the poor man's self control deserted him and he joined in the laughter that greeted my unwitting honesty!

Tiny also had to earn his living on the farm. During the early potato season he was harnessed to a trap and hauled baskets of potatoes up from the cliff meadows below Tregiffian. My job was to drive him up the path to the farmyard where one of the men unloaded the trap then I was lifted back and I drove Tiny down the path again for the next consignment.

There followed a succession of ponies and as I grew older, horses, some giving great pleasure, others frustration and disappointment but all contributing to experience. However, it was a young man called Jim and a book of poems which were really responsible for my first venture into the big, wide world. Jim Waters was a sergeant in the Australian army. We met him during the early years of the war. He came to stay on the farm through an organisation that had been devised to help entertain Commonwealth troops on leave in Britain. The idea was to provide places where troops could relax, a kind of 'home from home'. Some were Air Force boys, young, homesick and with nerves shattered by their experiences. Others were in the Australian army, perhaps spending their last few days of rest before being sent overseas. Jim was the first Australian we had ever met. We liked his cheerful, friendly personality. He told us that he owned a cattle station in a place called Corryong, situated near the Snowy River in Victoria. He had ridden all his life and won races on horses he had

Playing around on 'Tiny'

trained. Being a child still, I was greatly impressed by this young man with the bronzed face and strange accent and amazed by his description of horse breaking in the outback. "You mean you just slap a saddle on an unbroken colt and ride him straight away?" "Too right we do," he replied.- "and sometimes they go real crook."

Jim enjoyed riding round the farm and the novelty of jumping Cornish banks. When he left, like many other Australians whom we met, he said, "When the war is over you must come out to Australia and I will show you our country." Several of the others were unable to keep their promises – they died in the Phillipine jungles.

The war had been over for five years, when on that cold and blustery November day I returned from my ride on the cliffs to find that the postman had left a parcel with an Australian postmark for me. Jim had sent me a book of poems written by 'Banjo' Paterson, an Australian poet famous for his bush ballads and poems about the outback. Included was 'The man from Snowy River', a wonderfully descriptive poem which told the story of a young boy who out rides the finest horsemen in the country in a thrilling chase to recover a valuable racehorse that has escaped from its stable and joined a herd of 'brumbies' or wild horses.

Dad, sister Mary and I going hunting with the Western Hunt

Then fast the horsemen followed
Where the gorges deep and black
Resounded to the thunder of their tread
And the stockwhips woke the echoes
And they fiercely answered back
From cliffs and crags that beetled overhead …

The Snowy River country in which the epic ride takes place is only twelve miles from Jim's home. The description of the hunt through treacherous mountains reaches a climax when the boy catches the racehorse single handed.

….And he ran them single handed till their sides were white with foam
He followed like a bloodhound on their track
Till they halted, cowed and beaten; then he turned their heads for home
And alone and unassisted brought them back ….

I read the poem over and over again until I knew it by heart and had such a vivid picture in my mind that suddenly Jim's invitation to visit his home became irresistible and I decided there and then I was going to Australia.

✧ ✧ ✧

How easy it is to dream but how difficult to turn dreams into reality. I didn't realise the obstacles that would have to be overcome when I made my decision, nor the opposition that I would have to face. Nowadays we accept travelling round the world as commonplace but at that time Australia seemed a very long way away. Cornish people have always travelled, as typified by the old miner's wife from St. Just who when asked if she had ever been to Plymouth replied, "No, m'dear, we don't go nowhere – only to South Africa and back! My family was less than enthusiastic. "Whatever do you want to go there for? It's the other side of the world. You haven't any money." The last remark was certainly true and the greatest stumbling block to my plan. The following summer, however, that problem was solved in a most unexpected manner.

Mum with 'walked' hound puppy

Mary, dad and I judging, Kent County Show

Goldflake with one of her foals

Chapter 2: **Goldflake**

I think for most horse lovers who have a number of horses pass through their hands, there is invariably one that is remembered with special affection. It was a 14 hands 2ins. chestnut mare called Goldflake who will always have that particular place in my memory. I first met Goldflake on Penzance railway station. She had been sent down by train from Wales where she had been running virtually wild on the Brecon hills. My father had bought her while on holiday there. When the guard opened the door I saw a shivering, terrified pony cringing in the darkness of the truck. As she stepped timidly on to the platform I little realised the significant part that this sweating, bewildered little mare was going to play in launching me on my travels.

At that time she was an unbroken four year old and breaking her in turned out to be an affair beset with difficulties. She was highly strung and excitable and had a deep mistrust of human beings. Later, I found out that someone had tried to break her in but gave up when she became troublesome and turned her out on to the Welsh hills. Basically she was sweet tempered and affectionate and I spent long hours just riding her round the farm being painstakingly careful to avoid doing anything to frighten her. Nevertheless, it wasn't all a tale of sweet success; many times she came galloping back to the stable with an empty saddle, having bucked me off in the middle of some field.

Slowly, however, her confidence grew and eventually I believe that I had her complete trust. She became a successful show pony, and on one memorable occasion, ridden by Priscilla Hext, a well known horsewoman in Cornwall, even won a Ladies' Race at a local point-to-point. All these achievements still didn't endear her to my father who told me bluntly that if I intended to go to Australia she would have to be sold.

Cornish horse dealers, like the Irish, love doing a deal. There is a certain ritual that is invariably followed by both buyer and seller. Each assumes a façade of disinterest – the buyer pretending that he is not particularly keen on buying and the seller pretending that he doesn't really mind if he sells or not. Each cheerfully accepts the pretence in the other and knows it is all part of the game. Mr. X rings up the dealer and asks if he has a horse that might suit him. "I have just the horse," he replies – "but you had better come over and have a look at him pretty soon as I have someone else interested." There is always "someone else interested." A date is fixed and on the day selected for viewing, the horse in question is given extra exercise to settle him down before the prospective buyer arrives. Little blemishes are disguised by judicious use of a bit of boot polish; ewe necks are concealed by skilful plaiting and many other little tricks of the trade are employed in order to present the horse looking his best!

As he is led out, not by a flicker of an eye lash does Mr. X betray his interest. On the contrary, he tries to give the impression that, in fact, he is "… really looking for a bit more quality" – or "up to more weight" – or "with a little more bone." After having a ride on the horse he secretly decides to buy him but dismounts with an air of nonchalance as though he wasn't very impressed. "What is the lowest price you will take?" he asks. The dealer quotes a figure and adds, "I couldn't sell him for a penny less." Mr. X says that it is too much and pretends to leave, whereupon he is quickly invited in for a drink. Inside the house the subject is studiously avoided until Mr. X says he really must be going. As he walks through the door he suddenly turns to the dealer and says, as though it was an afterthought, "I'll tell you what I'll do. I will give you X pounds for your horse to take him off your hands." The dealer, having been offered more than he would have been pleased to accept, and, scenting victory, adds a tenner to the price offered and agrees to sell. Mr. X, in spite of the extra tenner, is delighted. He would have paid the original price asked if the dealer had insisted. As they shake hands, each has the satisfaction of thinking that he has "had a good deal!'

The sale of Goldflake, however, was a vastly different story. There was no sense of triumph or satisfaction. I hated the thought of selling her and couldn't believe, or rather did not want to believe that she would go quietly for anyone else. It was at a local horse show that a stranger came up to me and asked if the pony was for sale. At first my reply was a definite "No!" In spite of my father's ultimatum I could not face the thought of parting with her. "I am looking for a show pony for my 14 year old daughter and this one seems ideal," the stranger insisted. I pointed out that Goldflake was highly strung and not easy to ride. My comments merely produced the quick retort that his daughter was an accomplished rider. "I will give you £300 for the mare," he added. His offer astonished me, it was a fortune! In those days prices had not risen to the astronomical heights of today when a good show pony may fetch thousands of pounds. Still, I hesitated. The man raised his price to £325. I knew I would be foolish to turn down such an offer, especially as the money would more than finance my trip to Australia. The deal was made but I felt a traitor. Goldflake had come to trust me completely and I would be betraying that trust in handing her over to strangers of whom she was still wary and suspicious. I must admit, though, that lurking in the back of my mind was the thought that one day I would see her again as I had the feeling that she and her new owners would not understand one another.

I was right. Two weeks later I received a frantic telephone call from Maidenhead where Goldflake's new owners lived, informing me that the pony was wild and unrideable. Secretly I was gratified to think that she wouldn't go for anyone else but to redeem her character I offered to ride her in a show that was being held at Henley-on-Thames the following week. I hoped fervently she hadn't forgotten how to behave. I need not have worried. She won a strong class and ironically the judge commented on her good manners! Her character was redeemed. However, a few weeks later the telephone rang again. The girl still could not manage her. Would I take her back? It so happened that we had another, much quieter pony in the stables, so this was offered to the girl at the same price. The offer was accepted and Goldflake returned home. She was never sold again. She lived to be 21, having bred 8 foals, one of which became the mother of my mare, Manacle Mist, born in Coverack and died there, aged twenty five.

*Joan Laity
(now Howells)
on 'Timothy'
jumping for the
Cornish team at the
Bath & West show
1958*

Chapter 3. **Australia bound**

I often wonder if I would ever have seen Australia if Goldflake had not caught the eye of a wealthy man. With the money safely in the bank, I began to make definite plans for my departure. I thought it would be more interesting if I could share my adventure with a close friend and Joan Laity immediately sprang to mind. She was a distant cousin and we often spent part of our school holidays in each other's homes. She was a keen horsewoman and had won many prizes for show jumping so I rang and asked if she would like to go. I could picture her at the other end of the line; short dark hair, twinkling blue eyes – and now a very surprised look on her face. At first she thought I was joking but when I had convinced her I was serious she agreed to go.

We booked a passage on the P&O liner Maloja and waited eagerly for the sailing date. Alas it was not to be. The Korean War broke out and the whole idea was out of the question.

Our next attempt was made in January, 1952. The war in the east was over and once again we booked berths on the Maloja. A week before she was due to sail she developed engine trouble and our departure date was postponed. In this game of Snakes and Ladders we had dropped down to the tail of the snake yet again. My suitcase was packed and unpacked with increasing frustration until, at last, word from the shipping company shot us up to the top of the ladder – the Maloja would definitely be sailing on the 28th. February. We kept our fingers crossed and hoped!

On the morning of the 28th., even the drab Southampton docks failed to dampen my enthusiasm as I stood on the dockside and stared at the battered looking liner that was to take us 12,000 miles across the world. She reminded me of an old bath tub, with her peculiar rounded stern. The black paint on her hull was blistered and chipped – evidence of past struggles with a tempestuous sea. The Maloja was no oil painting but as I gazed at her ugly shape I forgave her lack of glamour – at that moment I would have cheerfully set sail in a bucket! After so many false starts it was difficult to believe we were actually on our way.

Our mothers had driven us up from Cornwall but sensibly decided not to wait until we sailed. We said our goodbyes quickly, avoiding the usual long drawn out farewells being shouted from the ship's rail. "Those holding British passports, please come this way." The polite voice interrupted my reverie and we were ushered aboard. We watched the gangway being removed and slowly, imperceptibly, the gap between ship and shore widened. On reflection, I realise that I have never again quite recaptured the excitement and emotion of that moment.

As on most ocean voyages, the first few days were spent on getting to know our fellow travellers. Most of them were emigrants. For many, as for Joan and me, it was the first time they had left the security of their homes. We were facing an unknown and uncertain future. Although the Maloja was one class only, the passengers soon sorted themselves into a pecking order. Some emerged as born organisers, trying to bully the more reticent into entering this or that competition with energetic but misplaced enthusiasm. Then there were the keep-fit fanatics who were to be found at six o'clock in the morning puffing and panting their way round and round the sports deck. At six o'clock in the evening they ruined all their efforts by propping up the bar and drinking themselves quietly into a maudlin state of inertia. Inevitably, there was the ship's bore. He was the predator. If he caught you sitting alone he would pounce like an eagle on its prey and regale you with oft repeated stories. Your only escape was to say, "Sorry, I have to go to the loo."

Many of the people whom we met are just hazy memories now but I still remember Jock, our little Scottish steward. When I told him I was feeling sick he said, "If ye are gonna be sick, eat dried rice – it's easier to clean up." I replied, "Don't worry – I've just eaten some nice fat pork!"

Romances blossomed on the poop deck. Some endured beyond the voyage, others were destined to fade away almost as soon as the ship reached her destination. During a game of deck tennis, Joan and I met two New Zealanders, Bill and Doug. They were about our own age. They had been working in England but we were the first Cornish people they had met. Some of our dialect expressions caused great hilarity and we were equally amused by some of theirs. I remember on one occasion as we were hurrying to go ashore I said, "C'mon, you two, you're always three scats behind." We couldn't help laughing at the perplexed expressions on their faces. Doug., however, got his own back when he referred to me as a 'drongo'. I didn't discover what 'drongo' meant until recently when I looked it up in an old dictionary. It said, 'A bird with an arched beak and a long forked tail!'

Our first port of call was Algiers. It was the first time I had visited a foreign city. The details have long since faded from my mind but I have never forgotten the shock of coming face to face with appalling, heart rending poverty. I shall never forget the children. Pathetic eyes stared helplessly from thin nut-brown faces.

Shabby, tattered clothes hung sadly from skinny little bodies. They looked at us with despondent resignation as though they expected nothing more from life. There were beggars too, sitting cross-legged on the baking pavements, their features lined with suffering and malnutrition. In contrast, I noticed some of the buildings were modern and well designed. Huge office blocks overlooked the harbour. To me, it seemed as if someone had built a modern city but had forgotten to clear up the human debris. Heat lay over the town like a thick blanket and there was a sweet smell in the air. We visited the Casbah, the famous native quarter. At that time, the women walked through the streets with their faces hidden behind veils, their white robes trailing in the dust.

Back on board ship, one day followed another in lazy enjoyment. The sun became hotter and the ship's officers shed their heavy winter uniforms for tropical whites. On the fourth day after leaving Algiers we sailed into the bay of Port Said. It was late in the afternoon and the buildings were silhouetted against a blazing sunset. The tall figure of Ferdinand de Lesseps, designer of the Suez Canal stood imposingly at the entrance to the harbour. Almost as soon as the noise of the Maloja's engines had ceased, we were besieged by Arab traders in scores of rowing boats which were laden with trinkets and souvenirs.

There was a rumour that we would not be allowed ashore. It was at the time of the political controversy of the canal. The Egyptians were trying to break Britain's control and British troops had been called in. I was disappointed but in the early evening some Egyptian Military Police came aboard and announced we could go ashore until ten o'clock provided we kept to certain areas. They stamped our passports and warned us that we must obey orders or they would not be responsible for our safety. The police escorted us ashore. As we shopped for souvenirs, armed guards stood at the entrances. The Egyptians in the streets stared at us defiantly but the shopkeepers tried to conceal their dislike behind ingratiating smiles, hoping we would buy something. We visited the famous Simon Artz store, bought some souvenirs and walked back through the warm, scented evening air to the security of the ship with a sense of relief.

The next day we steamed through the canal. British Army camps lined the banks and the troops waved and cheered as we nosed our way southwards. Behind the camps we could see a vast panorama of featureless sand. I noticed a lone figure kneeling. The Arab had turned his face towards the east, his camel was standing patiently beside him. Each morning the sun rose over the desert in a scarlet ball, growing paler as it increased in heat. By evening it again painted the sky in glorious shades of crimson, pink, purple and gold. We had been lucky so far; the sea had remained calm throughout the voyage, even the Bay of Biscay had failed to live up to its unpleasant reputation.

Two weeks after our departure from Southampton we reached Aden. We had little time to spend ashore in this dry, dusty town. The only thing I can remember about it is a camel! I thought it would be fun to have a photograph taken sitting on one. We came across a group of them in the market square, some standing quietly with their rough rope bridles knotted round their heads and others lying down, contentedly chewing their cud. Camels seem to be born with a perpetual look of disdain on their faces so I tried to find one which was a little less withering than the rest. I found one which looked docile enough. It had a basket strapped to its back. Gingerly I climbed into it and in a flash he leapt to his feet. I was helplessly marooned on the back of a very angry camel. Yells from some children playing nearby brought the astonished owner rushing into the square. He shook his fist and shouted at me as he grabbed the camel's rope. As I scrambled hastily out of the basket I thought it was just as well I couldn't understand what he was saying!

After Aden we headed out into the Indian Ocean. For days we saw nothing but an infinity of sea, with only the graceful flying fish for company. We anchored off Colombo on March 19th. It was siesta time when we went ashore. It was even hotter than Algiers and the natives lay sprawled in any bit of shade they could find with their heads cradled in their arms. I thought nothing could have been worse than the poverty we had seen in Algiers but here were children with hideous disfigurements holding up their begging bowls towards the tourists and lame, wrinkled old men chewing betel nuts with their hardened gums, spitting the juice into the gutter where it flowed like blood.

We watched a primitive bullock cart with iron rimmed wheels and a straw canopy being pulled along the street by two plodding oxen. Regardless of the siesta the rickshaw boys were looking for passengers. Joan and I decided to have a ride. Each rickshaw held one person and was drawn by a boy standing in the shafts like a horse. As I climbed in I noticed beads of perspiration on the ebony skin of the skinny little lad who was going to pull me. I felt uncomfortable. It suddenly seemed wrong that I should be sitting there while another human being struggled between the shafts like an animal. Across the road I saw a huge man who must have weighed about eighteen stone, sitting back in his rickshaw puffing at a cigar. The native pulling him looked old and frail and his passenger was yelling at him to go faster. He was doing his best but his client was dissatisfied. The spectacle sickened me. I could no longer enjoy my own ride so I asked the rickshaw boy to stop. I got out, gave him some money and walked away with a sense of shame.

In spite of the poverty in some quarters, Colombo possessed a charm and beauty that Algiers had lacked. Tall Palm trees lined the wide streets and in the gardens the white flowers of the Frangipani exuded that sweet, clinging fragrance which has become known as 'the smell of the east.' During the afternoon we visited a Buddhist temple where we were obliged to remove our shoes before entering. A large figure of Buddha dominated the building which was lavishly decorated with religious symbols. The temple's cool, dark interior was a welcome relief from the sticky heat and glare of the sun outside.

Before leaving England we had arranged to meet two students whom I had known during their course at the Cable and Wireless Engineering School at Porthcurno and were then stationed in Colombo. Later in the day they took us on a 'lightning tour' of the town, riding pillion on their motor bikes. Their description was apt. We saw 'the sights' through a haze of yellow dust as the road sped dizzily beneath our feet. The evening ended with a hilarious visit to a Chinese restaurant where we attempted to eat rice with chopsticks, taking so long that we only just managed to get back on board the Maloja before sailing time.

We crossed the Equator on March 21st. Being first timers, Joan and I were candidates for the usual initiation ceremony of 'Crossing the Line'. Some of the passengers dressed as King Neptune and his Courtiers and held the ceremony at the edge of the swimming pool. Those of us awaiting the 'royal' ducking were lined up and in turn asked to sit on a stool with our backs to the water. The 'King' then plastered our faces with a paste of flour and water after which we were obliged to drink something from a glass. Then we were bundled over backwards into the pool and ducked three times by two of the King's henchmen. The triple baptism entitled us to the coveted certificate.

We were now in the southern hemisphere and the appearance of the Southern Cross in the sky at night indicated we were nearing the end of our journey. There was an air of excitement on board. I often wonder what happened to those emigrants whose lives we had entered so briefly but had come to know quite well. We never saw them again.

It was on March 29th. that we sighted the blurred coastline of Australia. In the early morning a pale sun gradually brought it into focus and the buildings of Freemantle began to take shape. Dock areas are never the most attractive gateways to any country but the fact that we were about to set foot on Australian soil at long last gave this one an aura of charm. We went ashore in the early morning sunshine and as we had a few hours to spare we took the bus into Perth which was twelve miles away. There was little time to explore but in King's Park, perched high above the Swan River my Australian dream became reality. It is often the silliest little details that we remember and something which makes an impression on one person goes unobserved by another. I remember the taste of my first ice-cold pineapple milk shake, drunk in the shade of a gum tree while listening to the high pitched laugh of a kookaburra as it flew across the river. We saw a lyre bird with brilliantly coloured feathers, strutting in front of us as we walked in the park. Exotic flowers were blooming everywhere but they had no scent. Although it was nearing the Australian winter the sun blazed in a cloudless sky. Unfortunately we had no time to see anything else as we had to hurry back to the Maloja before she left for Adelaide. My first glimpse of Australia had been tantalisingly brief but like Keyhole Kate, that little peep made me want to see more.

Ploughing through the Australian Bight, the sea became very choppy and to my disgust I was seasick for the first time. It was a relief to get off the ship at Adelaide

Joan and I on Bondi beach

but I remember nothing about the city itself except that it was situated eighteen miles from the port. A terse entry in my diary for that day read, "Went into Adelaide by train. Cost: two shillings and nine pence. Had super meal at the Quality Inn including chocolate malted milkshakes." Milkshakes seem to have figured prominently on the whole Australian trip!

We were impatient now, wanting to reach Melbourne. We heard about the rivalry that exists between the residents of Melbourne and Sydney and had listened to the good-natured leg pulling between them on board ship. The Melbournian would taunt the man from Sydney: "Aw break it down, you Sydneysiders are all alike; you do nothing but drink beer and 'skite' about 'our harbour' and 'our bridge'". The man from Sydney would retort: "Yer reckon? You blokes have nothing but a racetrack and a bloody river that flows upside down" (The river Yarra that winds through Melbourne is, in some places, a dirty, muddy brown.) The latter well-worn remark never fails to rile a true Melbournian, who replies: "Sydney -huh- you call that heap of stones a city? No planning, no trees and goat tracks for streets. Yer stand six deep to wait for yer evening beer and fight fer a seat on the tram. Yer got no culture and no manners." Joan and I kept out of these arguments and waited to see them both for ourselves.

On April 4th. we landed in Melbourne. The Maloja was due to stay four days before ending her journey in Sydney, where we had arranged for friends to meet us. We now had time to explore the city and liked its wide, tree-lined avenues while enjoying souvenir hunting in the wide variety of shops. We visited the famous Flemington Racecourse, home of the Melbourne Cup. One day we went out into the Dandenong Ranges and gazed in awe at the golden Wattle which spread over the hills like rich, yellow butter. It was a dazzling sight and reminded me of the daffodil fields in Cornwall.

We left Melbourne in the late afternoon amid a chorus of 'goodbyes' from the crowd gathered on the jetty. Colourful streamers stretched from ship to shore and as we made our way slowly out to sea we were gradually engulfed in darkness while the flickering lights of the city dimmed to tiny pinpoints and finally disappeared.

Two days later we sailed into Sydney harbour. From the deck of the ship we could see the great arc of the Bridge clearly defined against a backcloth of brilliant blue sky. It was a thrilling sight but the excitement of coming to the end of our journey was tinged with nostalgia. We had heard that this was the Maloja's last voyage – her next journey would be to the breakers' yard. As we walked down the gangplank for the last time, we looked back at the rather shabby old ship with real affection and silently thanked her for bringing us safely across 12,000 miles of ocean.

Cattle ranching in Australia

Chapter 4: **Travels down under**

From the moment we stepped ashore at Sydney Joan and I were engulfed in friendly hospitality. There to meet us were three girls whom we already knew; they had all stayed at Bosistow in 1950. Paulette Shehadie was the sister of Nick Shehadie whom we had met in Penzance when he came over to play rugby for the Wallabies touring team in 1947. He was later to become Lord Mayor of Sydney. Then there was Ethel Cornieluissen whose family originated from Norway and finally, Norma Graham who lived near Bondi Beach and it was to her home that we were invited to spend the first few days in Australia.

The highlight of those few days was a visit to the Royal Sydney Easter Show. It was a spectacular affair but not at all what I had expected. There was none of the formality of our own Royal Show. The atmosphere was very free and easy; commentators called each other by their Christian names and cracked jokes over the loudspeaker. Most of the classes were sponsored by commercial firms who advertised their goods as the classes were announced. – "Class 5, ladies and gentlemen will be the Open Jumping. Ladies! Do you wake up in the morning feeling tired and listless? You do? Then take X's Tonic." Although it sounded strange to us, it was an excellent way of advertising.

The main ring was enormous, with a circular track skirting the perimeter on which trotting races were held at frequent intervals. The horse classes at that time were very different from those at British Shows. For instance, the hacks were divided into 10, 12 and 14 stone categories. They came into the ring with unplaited manes and bushy tails. The elegant competitors in England would have raised aristocratic eyebrows at such laxity. On the whole the hacks lacked quality – the judges seemingly preferred bone and substance.

We only managed to see one jumping class which was termed 'a hunting event'. The riders wore racing silks and the fences were built of heavy timber. The horses, ridden in plain snaffle bridles, galloped flat out from start to finish! The Camp Drafting competitions were a unique test of skill and precision. The rider was required to select a bullock from a pen, cut it out from the rest of the herd, drive it between certain flags and then return it to the pen.

The Buckjumping events were the ones that thrilled me most of all. Horses with graphic names such as Red Demon, Wildfire, Satan and Killer erupted from the chutes in a twisting, writhing whirlwind of horseflesh that must have jarred every bone in the rider's body. Some horses threw themselves into the air with ears laid back and nostrils flared, kicking up a cloud of dust as they landed. With each shattering buck they ducked their heads between their knees in desperate attempts to dislodge their riders. A few reared and then plunged forward in wild bounds – contortions that would have sent any ordinary rider into orbit but these men stuck like leeches, their bodies swaying with each violent movement. The rules demanded that one hand must be held high above the head while the other held the halter rope. The competitor was judged by the number of bucks he could withstand in eight seconds. If he was still on board after that time, another rider would gallop alongside, release a bucking strap and snatch him off. Then he would ride out of the ring behind his rescuer. Occasionally a contestant would be caught off balance and there would be a hiss of indrawn breath as the spectators watched him being flung high into the air. Most of the competitors landed unhurt but now and then one would land awkwardly and either hobble out of the ring or be carried off on a stretcher.

The final parade of the Show was a most impressive spectacle. The prize-winners formed into concentric circles and revolved round the centre of the enormous ground. Each class was represented and they presented a kaleidoscope of colour and movement.

Following our visit to the Royal Show the three girls took it in turn to entertain us. With typical Australian hospitality we were shown so much in the space of a week that our faces became creased in permanent grins of approval. A hotchpotch of memories come crowding back as I write … I remember the lifesaving teams at work on the beaches of Bondi, Cogee and Manly – in particular a small boy whom we saw dragged from the thundering surf – Rugby matches and a clear young voice carrying across the pitch, "Take your b….dy foot away from my face" and an angry retort, "Take your bloody face away from my foot!" The Blue Mountains; a carpet of grey sheep moving slowly along a track; bleached grass and naked white Gum trees silhouetted against an evening sky; the silence of the bush – only an hour's journey from the clanging trams of Sydney. I remember too, invitations to 'tea' when we arrived at four o'clock to find that tea in Australia means supper. Trips into the outback; boiling water in a billy can over an open fire; finding an old, derelict goldfield and imagining we could see a tiny, sparkling pinpoint in a lump of mud. We were introduced to relatives, friends and friends of friends and sampled the hospitality of a great many Australian homes. We went to dances that today would be considered old fashioned. We learned how to do the 'Gypsy Tap' and the 'Jolly Miller' which is the Australian version of our 'Paul Jones.'

By the end of that first fortnight we had used up all the words of appreciation in our vocabulary and were becoming exhausted by too many late nights and so much to do and see. Joan and I decided it was time for a rest and take a short period on our own. We flew from Sydney to Canberra. The journey took an hour and a half and we had a wonderful bird's eye view of the snow capped Australian Alps and Mount Kosciusko, the highest mountain in Australia. Canberra's history is an interesting one. The name is derived from an aboriginal word meaning 'meeting place.' It was a deliberate man-made capital, unlike most cities which grow naturally from their geographical position and the needs of the inhabitants. The rivalry between Melbourne and Sydney, with each demanding the prestige of being the capital became so intense that the government decided to build a city half way between the two. Designs were invited and architects from all over the world submitted their blue prints. Finally an American named Walter Griffin was given the responsibility of planning the capital. It was a simple, yet original plan, with the Houses of Parliament in the centre and the streets radiating from them like the spokes of a wheel.

When Joan and I paid our flying visit in 1952, Canberra was still being built. It was a strange, immature capital where flocks of sheep were apt to wander in the streets and the high pitched call of the kookaburra perched in nearby gum trees was louder than the traffic! It seemed as though the great trackless bush of Australia was loath to give up its title and still lay in wait at the gates of the city. Our few days in Canberra gave us a chance to recuperate from the generous hospitality in Sydney. I was eagerly looking forward to meeting Jim again and visiting his home at Corryong near the Snowy River. I remembered Banjo Paterson's description of the countryside in his poem –

> "And down by Kosciusko where the pine-clad ridges raise
> Their torn and rugged battlements on high,
> Where the air is clear as crystal and the white stars blaze
> At midnight in the cold and frosty sky …"

We left Canberra in the early morning. Travelling by coach afforded an opportunity to see some of the country and it wasn't long before we realised the vastness of the place, finding it staggering that one could travel for a hundred miles without a change of scenery. At one stage we drove through an area where bush fires had raged the previous year. The devastation was unbelievable. Blackened tree stumps littered the ground and ghostly white tree trunks with branches twisted like bare bones leaned drunkenly. The tinder-dry grass, crisp and brown, failed in places to cover sooty patches of earth. Yet, in the midst of such shocking desolation, there were unexpected flashes of beauty. Little parrot-like rosellas with brilliantly coloured feathers flitted among the dead branches, adding a touch of enchantment to an otherwise macabre countryside.

As we drove deeper into the bush the roads deteriorated, becoming little more than potholed tracks. Our coach driver, who had a lively sense of humour said, "If you ever drive a car along this road you'd better blow your horn when you come to a pothole." "Why?" we asked innocently. "Because there might be another car already in it," he replied with a grin. Roads in Australia have been greatly improved since we were there, of course; however our irrepressible driver taught us a song which we sang to the tune of Galway Bay.

"If you ever take a bus ride down to Melbourne
You need only pay half fare the drivers say,
You'll be bumped up in the air so blinkin' often
You'll only occupy the seats half way.
For the farmers never churn their milk in Canberra,
They've got a better method so they say,
They just put it on the bus that runs to Melbourne
And it's butter long before it gets half way!"

The road we were on went through Albury then on down to Melbourne where Jim had arranged to meet us. I wondered if I would recognise him after ten years. He hadn't changed. I knew him instantly as we stepped off the bus. He introduced us to Kath, his attractive wife, then explained they had been on holiday in Melbourne and were going to drive us the three hundred miles to their home. The route would take us along the Hume Highway to Albury, where we would branch off and travel another hundred miles to Corryong. Distance means nothing in Australia but to me it seemed as if we drove for an eternity through a rather parched countryside. As we approached Corryong however, the grass became greener and the gum trees were in full leaf. The road threaded its way through the hills until suddenly we saw the Snowy River glinting in the sunlight. As I watched the glistening water, another scene flashed into my mind; a windy cliff top with waves crashing against the rocks on the day I had made up my mind that I was going to Australia. Now, incredibly, here I was, actually looking at the Snowy River and the mountains and valleys which Banjo Paterson had made immortal. I was not disappointed. His graphic description was no illusion.

Jim's home, Tarqua, was a white, weatherboard house, built beside a clear creek. Weeping Willows drooped over the water and tall Poplars screened the house from the road. In the distance there was a range of grape-blue mountains, with Mount Kosciusko towering above the others, its snow-capped summit vanishing into the clouds. By Australian standards, Tarqua was a small station. A herd of sixty Jersey cows, which Jim milked on his own and a larger herd of Red Poll beef cattle. At that time, Jim and Kath had two children, Campbell, a fair haired boy with mischievous blue eyes and his twin sister Jenny, who was dark eyed and brunette. They were about four years old and a lively, lovable pair..

At Tarqua it was easy to forget the outside world. In this isolated, serene and beautiful country of cattle and gum trees and an everlasting blue sky, we found it difficult to believe that anything else existed. There were no other houses for miles – Corryong itself was four miles away. No tradesmen called; the baker left bread in a tin drum at the end of the stony lane leading up to the house and Jim collected his mail from Corryong three times a week. It was branding time while we were there and we rode the hardy little stock ponies up into the mountains to round up the strays. It was exciting, exhilarating work, the ponies knowing much more about the job than we did. They galloped after the cattle like dogs chasing cats but they were sure-footed and very fast. Jim warned us to beware of wombat holes. These small, beaver-like animals dig deep burrows that are a danger to a galloping horse. One morning we saw hundreds of cockatoos, snow white with yellow crests, settle on one of the paddocks. To us it was a lovely sight but the farmers are unappreciative of their beauty as they damage the crops, especially wheat.

A unique feature of Australian bush life is the Picnic Race Meeting. These races are held on the flat for amateur riders only and members of the Picnic Race Clubs. At Holbrook, not far from Corryong, their meetings are traditionally held on the first Friday in May. By lucky chance a meeting was being held during our stay at Tarqua and Jim kindly offered to take us. The scene when we arrived was typical of the happy, friendly and informal attitude of the Australian sporting fraternity. Families sat on the grass eating sandwiches and drinking beer while the bookies set up their boards and prepared for business. Jim explained that the races were divided into two sections, one for grass fed horses and the other for those that had been stabled. The former had to comply with certain rules. Six weeks before the date of the meeting all the runners in this section are put into paddocks supervised by a member of the committee and are fed on grass only. Three weeks prior to the race they are returned to their owners who can then train them as they please. There are no cash prizes, just trophies, however, an unusual feature of Picnic Racing is the Calcutta Sweepstake, which is held on the evening before the meeting. It is open to members and guests only. The names of the runners are put into a hat and lots are drawn. If you draw a horse you can bid for it. If it wins you then get a percentage of the pool money.

We went down to the paddock. Some of the horses looked as if they had come straight in from mustering cattle, with their untrimmed manes blowing in the breeze but each one seemed hard and fit. I saw a few arrive on the course in an open truck, their heads hanging unconcernedly over the side – a sight that would have made an English trainer turn pale! Jim had an unexpected treat in store for me. Apparently he had gone to endless trouble to find a ride for me in the Ladies' Race and eventually managed to persuade a friend of his to let me ride one of his horses.

I shall never forget my brief but exciting few moments as a flat race jockey. It was obligatory to wear racing silks so I had to borrow the owner's. They were pale blue with gold sleeves and a gold cap. Jim's boots and breeches done up in a few strategic places with safety pins completed the outfit. The minimum weight for the Ladies' Race was ten stone, so as I was only eight, I had to carry a lot of lead. I didn't have a chance to look at the horse I was to ride until he was walking round

Riding 'Gold Sard' at the Holbrook Picnic Races. Australia.

the paddock. He was dark brown, about 15.2 hh and I can still remember his bridle. It must have been made of nylon because it was white and looked most attractive against his dark head. There were eight runners. All the other girls looked very professional in their jockey attire. As the bell went for the 'jockeys up' I hurriedly adjusted my leathers. The owner had warned me that the horse, whose name was Gold Sard, hated facing the tapes and would probably back away. As the race was only a four furlong sprint I had visions of being left at the post! We cantered sedately enough down to the start but I could feel Gold Sard taking a firm hold and he was beginning to break out into a sweat. The favourite was a horse called Resgras, a big, racing sort and I eyed him warily as we lined up for the roll call. In the mêlée of excited horses it was difficult to keep mine facing the right way and he backed nervously away from the tapes. Suddenly they shot up and we were launched into a tidal wave of coloured silks, flaring nostrils, waving manes and pounding hooves. Gold Sard was taken by surprise and hemmed in by the other horses had no alternative but to go with them. We were half way up the course before I realised that most of the field were behind us. Resgras was a long way in front but at the two furlong post we found ourselves battling it out for second place with a horse called Greenlaw I could see his nose creeping past my horse's flank but little Gold Sard had done his best and Greenlaw passed the winning post a length ahead. I was thrilled to come third, nevertheless and grateful to Jim for giving me a unique experience.

Sadly, our holiday at Tarqua was over. Jim and Kath and family had given us a wonderful time and we reluctantly waved goodbye. I took a last look at the Snowy Mountains and half expected to see …

On a dim and distant hillside
The wild horses racing yet
With the man from Snowy River
At their heels.

A few days later we were on our way to Queensland. The Pioneer Tour Company had planned a trip for us which would last a month and included a boat trip to the Great Barrier Reef, a tour of Northern Queensland and visits to the principal cities and towns on the east coast. I usually dislike organised coach trips but we wanted to see as much of Queensland as we could in the shortest time and the best way of doing it was by going on a tour. Cities and towns have never held much interest for me but I enjoy the changing scenery of the countryside. Queensland was rich in tropical vegetation. We drove through acres of pineapples, paw-paws, passion fruit and mangoes. Coconuts and bananas grew by the wayside and giant ferns spread their fronds in a jungle of green lace. At one stage the driver pointed to a plant with long, spiked leaves – "Now, that is the Gympie, folks and for the benefit of any sticky beak on the coach who may want to touch it, don't. I'm warning yer, it's deadly poison." Apparently many an unwary traveller in the pioneering days had died after pricking his finger on it. The country was ablaze with colour; the brilliant scarlet of the poinsettias, Queensland's national flower; the purple bougainvilleas, mauve jacaranda and a vast assortment of tropical shrubs and plants. We broke off sticks of sugar cane to chew and picked wild raspberries by the roadside. We were introduced to houses built on stilts and slept in beds with mosquito nets draped round them that gave us a sense of claustrophobia. We mentioned it and were told, "My oath, you pommies are ignorant. Yer wont suffocate if yer pull the nets tight . They let the air in and keep the skeeters out!"

Just off Brisbane, on Lone Pine Island, we saw koala bears in their natural surroundings; cuddly little balls of fluff, either asleep or stripping the gum leaves. Six hundred miles north of Brisbane we reached Mackay. From this busy little town we hired a fifty foot launch to take us on a tour of the Barrier Reef. The Silver Wake was owned by a young Australian couple, Rex and Vi. They earned their living by hiring out their boat to tourists. They did the crewing themselves with the assistance of a young, good looking blond haired man called Pete who combined the duties of First Mate, Deckhand and Chief Guide. Apart from Joan and me there were only two other passengers; an elderly grey-haired man whom we affectionately called "Pop", and his son Ernie. They were farmers, owners of a dairy farm in Gippeland, Victoria. The old man had long cherished a dream that one day he would take a holiday away from the farm and see for himself the Great Barrier Reef about which he had read and heard so much. We had met on the quayside and were soon aboard the Silver Wake and heading out to sea. For a week we lost all sense of time, no newspapers, no radio, nothing to remind us of the outside world. We cruised slowly and lazily among the palm-fringed islands of the Coral Sea. At night we anchored off a beach, ivory white in the moonlight and rowed ashore in the dory. As we waded barefoot through the warm softly lapping waves, our feet left a phosphorescent trail of dancing lights in the water. We visited Daydream, Pentecost, South Mole and the Brampton Islands. As it was now June, in the Australian winter, we had these lovely islands almost to ourselves. From a glass bottomed boat we looked down into the mysterious, technicoloured depths of the sea and saw a wonderland. Coral had formed into all kinds of shapes and colours and tropical fish with vivid rainbow colours darted here and there, contrasting sharply with the jet black sea urchins. Although it was enchanting we were reminded of the incongruity of nature when we saw an ugly giant clam with its gaping mouth, waiting to pounce on an unwary victim.

It was a lazy, idyllic week. We fished, swam, sunbathed and watched tropical sunsets that were indescribable in their sheer magnificence. The evening before we were due to return to Mackay, Pete called me up on deck and asked, "Have yer ever seen anything like this? Yer just wouldn't read about it, would yer?" I must admit, I was speechless. Looking westwards, the whole sky glowed a deep, fiery red and great streaks of dark purple were gathering on the horizon. As the sun dipped lower, the brilliant colours softened but the dark clouds moved nearer. There was an eerie stillness in the air. The Coconut palms silhouetted against the sky were motionless. We had anchored for the night on the leeward side of one of the uninhabited islands but there was no feeling of safety. The darkness held a threat.

At daybreak it began to rain. We weighed anchor and headed for the harbour at Mackay. As we left the lee of the island, the storm broke. The sea, which on the previous evening had been glassily calm, now boiled and hissed round our bows, tossing the Silver Wake from one wave to another. One moment we were hovering on the crest, the next we were diving into a huge black trough. I was convinced the boat was going to split in half, she seemed too small and frail to withstand such a savage battering. As she pitched and rolled, the port and starboard rails were alternately under water. We held on to the nearest fixture and watched in horror as the gigantic mounds of water built up in front of us. Rex the Skipper clung to the wheel and as the gale hit us with the fury of a wild cat a deluge of rain hit the decks. Miraculously we stayed afloat but I began to wonder how much longer we could survive. After half an hour the storm abated. We limped into the harbour at Mackay, white-faced and shaken and never more thankful to find solid ground under our feet.

After that experience the rest of the tour was somewhat of an anti-climax. We continued our journey northwards along the east coast through Townsville and Cairns to Cooktown where we literally came to the end of the road. At that time, the coastal road petered out at that point. The end of the road had come for Joan and me too. Our Australian visit was nearly over. We travelled by train back to Sydney where we stayed with more friends, then we went on to Melbourne from where we were due to leave for home on the Orontes of the Orient Line. Some of Joan's relatives lived in Melbourne. The older generations had not lost their Cornish accents. A love of Cornwall was still evident in their voices as they spoke nostalgically of the old days. It was strange to be among people with such Cornish names as Berriman and Kitchen. Home seemed very near. The departure from Melbourne was very different from the sober leave-taking at Southampton. The docks were thronged with chattering, excited people. Gay streamers were thrown from ship to shore. A band played 'Now is the Hour' as we left harbour. On deck, I watched Australia gradually disappear with mixed feelings. I was sorry to be saying goodbye to all the kind people we had met and to be closing my Australian diary but I was already looking forward to the first sight of England – and home.

Mrs Vinicky and I giving a High School demonstration at Clanfield near Portsmouth.

Mrs Vinicky on Kordofan and me on Neapolitano

Chapter 5: **High School horses**

'Large streams from little fountains flow,
Tall oaks from little acorns grow.'

Two years after my return from Australia I was reminded of this well known quotation when an incident occurred, trivial enough at the time but it was eventually to lead to an interesting and unusual experience. Eileen Laity, an aunt of mine, who lived near Lelant gave me a copy of 'Sport and Country' in which was an article she knew might interest me. It concerned a new riding school that had been recently opened at Wolvercote, just outside Oxford. It was owned jointly by an Englishman named Organ and a Czech couple, Mr. and Mrs. Vinicky who were well known High School riders and had performed in most of the continental circuses. In 1943 Mr. Vinicky was running a large riding school in Prague but when the Russians took over, he and his wife escaped by joining a circus bound for Sweden. They stayed there until 1948 when they came to England. Here, they met Mr. Organ who had always been interested in horses and between them they decided there was an opening in this country for a school that specialised in Dressage and Haute Ecole. The Vinickys had managed to bring their six fully trained High School horses with them. Mr. Vinicky had also made a name for himself through training dogs, polar bears, zebras, camels and elephants. He was also the only man ever to train a troupe of Highland bulls to perform in the circus ring. The article went on to explain that Pat Smythe had been invited to open the school, named 'The Lawn School of Equitation.' The Sport and Country illustrations showed a spacious indoor school, stabling for between twenty and thirty horses and a junior jumping arena that overlooked 300 acres of flat grassland skirting the River Thames. It looked superb. On impulse I wrote to the Vinickys, asking for a job. As luck would have it, their head girl was getting married so I was invited to come for an interview. Fortunately I was accepted and a few weeks later I had found lodgings nearby and was working at the Lawn

School, helping with the instruction, schooling young horses and learning how to ride a High School horse.

At that time, Mr. Vinicky began to suffer from bouts of arthritis which got steadily worse until he was forced to give up riding. Sadly, the 'Josi and Manja Double High School Act' was brought to an end. The pair had performed in theatres, on TV and at many horse shows. They had been booked to give demonstrations at various functions during the coming summer months and to my surprise, Mr. Vinicky asked me if I would take his place at an Exhibition near Bristol. Although feeling sorry for him, I was delighted to think I was being given a chance to realise a secret ambition. I remembered the times, as a child, when I had sat impatiently through circus programmes, waiting eagerly for the High School rider to appear, dreaming that one day I would ride in a circus.

On the day of the Exhibition I travelled with the horses to Bristol in the Vinickys' enormous horse box which had 'Vinickys' High School Horses' written across the front. Mrs. Vinicky was to ride a little golden dun Andalusian stallion called Kordofan and I had Neapolitano, a grey Lipizzaner stallion which had previously been Mr. Vinicky's mount and was an experienced circus horse. We had been engaged to do four performances at 3 pm and 8 pm on two consecutive days. It seems extraordinary in this day and age that at that time our music was to be provided by gramophone records, a man being detailed to change the tunes at the appropriate moments!

Just before 3 pm on the first day, all was ready. Mrs. Vinicky was wearing a maroon outfit of a fitted jacket, a long flowing divided skirt and a plumed tricorn hat. As I was standing in for her husband I was dressed in a bluish-grey tail coat, with a white shirt, black bow tie and top hat. Both horses had blue bandages on their forelegs. The arena was a roped off enclosure in the centre of the Fairground. The man in charge of the music sat with the needle poised over the turntable as he waited for us to begin. At a sign from us, the 'Surrey with the fringe on top,' the jaunty tune from Oklahoma, echoed through the loudspeakers and the horses, with ears pricked, trotted side by side into the ring. For better or worse, I was a High School rider at last! Our performance began with various movements at the trot. First was the Travers in which the horse moves obliquely sideways with his head towards the outside of the arena and slightly bent in the direction of the movement. This was followed by the Renvers, a similar lateral movement but this time with the head towards the inside of the arena. We then took the horses into the centre of the ring where they pawed the air in unison with their near forelegs. Continuing the trot tempo, we then performed half passes (more lateral movements) across the arena from right to left and vice versa. A change of music followed and to a stirring march we did the Spanish Walk, an impressive movement in which the horse lifts his front legs as high as possible in the form of a goose step. Another change of tempo and with the three beat rhythm of the canter to the tune of the 'Teddy Bears' Picnic,' we did the change of leg at every four, three, then two strides. This was followed by circus pirouettes where the circle is reduced until the horse canters around literally in his own length with his hind legs marking time on the spot while his fore legs canter round them. The final was the polka, a three beat movement which we did side by side and followed it with the spectacular elevated trot of the 'Passage.' We ended the Double High School act with the horses dropping down on one knee in a graceful bow.

After the double act we each contributed a solo. Mrs. Vinicky had taught Kordofan to do the Rumba, which he performed in such a cheeky manner that the applause of the crowd was ringing out even before he had finished. My solo act on Neapolitano was a Piaffe, where the horse does an elevated trot on the spot without gaining ground. Although I had practised it many times before, I had never ridden it to music but the effect was entrancing. It felt as if the horse was dancing on a trampoline; the controlled suspension between each step in perfect time to the music gave me a feeling of weightlessness as though we were puppets on a string. The Piaffe ended with the Levade, a form of half rear and the classical stance of the charger that is often seen on memorial plinths.

The following day we almost had a disaster. There was a howling gale and the pile of gramophone records was blown over. When they had been restacked, they were put in the wrong order and as Neapolitano began his dignified Piaffe, the music blared into a jigging Rumba. There was a burst of laughter from the spectators, followed by a cheer as the poor red-faced man in charge eventually found the correct music!

Major Ferguson's stables near Windsor Park

Chapter 6: **Polo interlude**

Some time after our return from Bristol, Mr. Vinicky was finding it increasingly difficult to carry on at the Lawn School. His arthritis was growing steadily worse so one day Mr. and Mrs. Vinicky told me they would be leaving, taking their High School horses with them. I thought that was the end of my brief career as a High School rider so I returned to Cornwall.

At about that time I noticed an advertisement in Horse and Hound for a girl groom to work with polo ponies. It was from Major Ferguson, father of The Duchess of York. He was a member of the Windsor Park polo team. Knowing nothing about polo, I decided to try and learn something about this unfamiliar branch of horsemanship and applied for the job. I was asked to go to London for an interview which fortunately turned out to be successful. I started work in a lovely little private yard near Windsor Park. It was run by a very strict, meticulous stud groom whose name was John John. Digs were found for me about a mile away from the stable and I remember pedalling to work on a bicycle at six o' clock every morning. My wages were £3 10s. per week, plus food and accommodation.

Working with polo ponies was a completely new experience and one which, though I had no inkling of it at the time, was to lead me across the Atlantic for the second time. Major Ferguson owned some of the best international ponies in Britain and it was a pleasure to ride these beautifully schooled animals. The word 'polo' is derived from a Tibetan word, 'pulu' meaning ball. Organised polo came to this country in 1868 but primitive forms of the game were played in China and Japan more than a thousand years ago. England acquired the game via India as the sport's pioneers were the army officers and tea planters who had learned to play on the hard, sun-drenched pitches of India. The height limit of polo ponies in 1895 was increased from 14.00 hands to 14.2, and in early 1900's was abolished altogether. Today, the term 'pony' is misleading as some of them are almost hunters. In any polo game, especially the important Cup Matches, the role of the groom is vital. He or she must ensure that each pony is fit and absolutely sound; that the tack is correctly adjusted; that all bandages and boots are secure and that the stirrup leathers are the exact length for the rider. Once the game has started it is not stopped for any reason other than an accident and every second is precious. If a player wants to change his pony during a game, another one must be waiting on the sidelines and as he has no time to adjust his own leathers he relies on the forethought of the groom. Polo sticks vary in length according to the height of the pony. The groom must know which stick is used by the rider of each animal. If one is broken, another must be available immediately.

As soon as each seven and a half minute chukka is over the pony is brought back to the lines where he is sponged down, scraped and dried, then led round to cool off. Legs have to be inspected carefully and cuts and bruises tended on the spot. The whole pattern of a polo game is fast and furious and a moment of neglect by a groom can be as depredating to victory as a mistake by a player on the field. The riders, especially during international matches, are under great strain and an incompetent groom can be the last straw.

The Windsor Park team was captained by Prince Philip. I have vivid memories of him during practices on Smith's Lawn, galloping full tilt towards the pony lines, making unprintable remarks about his pony's hard mouth. There are memories of the Queen also, with a headscarf tied casually round her hair, chatting happily to players and grooms alike.

The work was hard but always interesting. There were no set hours – practices took place whenever the players could get together. Matches were sometimes played late in the day which meant that we were often working until midnight. Major Ferguson owned five ponies. I looked after three of them and John the other two. The stable management was of a very high standard. Both ponies and premises had to be immaculate at all times. We even plaited the straw at the entrance to each box to make them look neat and tidy! The ponies were exercised for about two hours every day except on the mornings following a match when they were led out to graze for half an hour. They were fed on best quality oats and chaff and hay and bran mashes once or twice a week together with an occasional handful of carrots. The job involved a certain amount of travelling when we visited other parts of the country to play in various tournaments. I still remember some of the hilarious parties in the tack room after a game when we drank champagne from paper cups to celebrate a notable win!

At the conclusion of the polo season I went home to roost and as I thought, settle down to some work on the farm…

Off to Smith's Lawn for polo practice

*'Ziggy' doing his
favourite party piece!*

Chapter 7: **Sequins and sawdust**
Cirkus Scott and Strassburger

The telegram arrived at lunchtime.

I had been home for almost twelve months when it arrived completely out of the blue. It read, "Please come immediately. Stop. Badly need rider for High School Act. Stop. Letter follows." It was signed Vinicky and the address was Sweden.

The next day a letter arrived, explaining that they had taken their horses to Sweden and were working for a Swedish circus called 'Cirkus Scott.' Mrs. Vinicky and two girls had been performing a triple High School Act, but one of the girls had left suddenly and as they were under contract to provide three riders, a replacement had to be found as quickly as possible. Already they had travelled as far as Umea on the east coast and were booked to perform in Lapland and the Arctic Circle. Mrs. Vinicky required an immediate answer.

My reply was both immediate and brief – "Am on my way."

There followed a few days of feverish activity, checking timetables, booking tickets and gathering together the clothes I would need, but in what seemed an amazingly short time I was on the Cornish Riviera, puffing its way to Paddington. At Harwich I boarded the 'Kronprinz Frederick' and after a choppy crossing to Esbjerg, caught a train to Copenhagen. As we sped across Denmark I remember thinking how patriotic the Danes must be as in almost every front garden of the tiny white-washed houses which dotted the countryside, their national flag was flying.

I arrived in Stockholm to find that I had a dreary wait of three hours before the night train left for Umea. In the crowded waiting room there was a buzz of conversation and I felt very much alone amid the strange jumble of, to me,

'Ziggy' again!

unintelligible words. Soon after midnight the train arrived but as I made myself comfortable in the sleeping car, I knew that sleep was far away; I was too excited at the prospect of what lay ahead.

We reached Umea early in the morning. As I stepped on to the small, deserted platform it began to rain. The station roof glistened as the drops splattered the slates and my suitcase was becoming saturated as I hurried towards the exit. A grim-faced ticket collector hardly looked up when I handed him the soggy little square of cardboard. Outside I saw a row of black taxis. I walked up to the first driver and asked to be taken to Cirkus Scott. A look of bewilderment crossed his face. I repeated 'Cirkus Scott'. He shook his head slowly from side to side. This time I said more loudly, as if by shouting I would force him to understand, "Do you know where the circus is?" He looked completely blank. In those few seconds I really understood the immensity of a language barrier. He shrugged his shoulders and we stood glaring at each other while the rain trickled down the back of my neck. I could feel it soaking through the jacket of my suit. I repeated the words, "Cirkus Scott" very carefully and deliberately. Suddenly his face broke into an enormous grin, "Ah, Cirkus Scott, ya, ya." The light had dawned and I scrambled thankfully into the taxi. We drove along a wide avenue lined with silver birches. I noticed hundreds of bicycles propped against the pavements. The shops looked prosperous, particularly the delicatessens which were stacked high with rich, creamy-looking cakes and pastries – a sight which literally made my mouth water. Within a few moments we had turned off the main street and there in the distance I caught my first glimpse of the Big Top of Cirkus Scott, its blue canvas being washed by the rain.

As the taxi pulled up outside the gate I guessed that the site must be some kind of recreation ground as there were children's swings and roundabouts in a corner of the field. Red caravans stood in symmetrical lines. A long tent had been erected next to the Big Top into which I saw a man leading a horse. I paid the driver and stood for a moment staring at this strange scene. All the tents and caravans seemed to be arranged in a definite pattern although some of them had not yet sprung to life. A few tents still lay in a sodden mass of canvas, ropes and pegs. There were men everywhere, shouting instructions to each other in guttural voices which I presumed were German. Some wore old sou'westers, others had fur-lined jackets with hoods hiding their faces, giving them rather a sinister appearance. They were busily hammering pegs into the oozing mud and fixing electric cables to the roofs of the caravans.

As I stood with my feet gradually sinking into the quagmire, feeling cold, hungry and very lonely, I asked the nearest man where I might find Mr. Vinicky. He didn't understand a word. We were back to the old language problem. I walked towards the line of red caravans and suddenly caught sight of Mr. Vinicky waving to me. I heaved a sigh of relief. It was good to see someone I knew and to hear English spoken, albeit in a broken accent. Mrs. Vinicky came to the door of their caravan and gave me a smiling welcome. After a steaming hot cup of coffee and a change into dry clothes, I was soon feeling better. The Vinicky's caravan, or living wagon as circus folk call it, was   divided into two sections. The couple lived on one side and the other half was allocated to the German girl, who was to complete the riding trio, and myself. The two halves were entirely separate. I was introduced to Ulrika, an attractive girl with a rosy complexion and bright blue eyes but her expression was petulant and looked as if she seldom laughed. When the rain stopped the drab scene that greeted me on arrival was transformed. The sun came out and women began to emerge from their wagons to hang up their washing or go shopping. By this time all the tents had been erected and Mrs. Vinicky took me over to see the horses. There was dear old Neapolitano – 'Nappy' to his friends – the Lipizzaner I had ridden at Oxford who was now Mrs. Vinicky's mount. Next to him stood Bellornato which the Vinickys had bought from the Spanish Riding School in Vienna. He was slightly bigger than Nappy who was only 15.2 hh but had the same placid temperament, I was told. Ulrika was to ride him. My mount, Ziglary, known to all as 'Ziggy,' was the smallest of the three/ He was only 14.3 hh but with his beautifully chiselled head and dished face he looked more like an Arab than a Lipizzaner. He was the fiery one of the trio and his enormous brown eyes looked alert and eager. All three were stallions but they stood quietly tied up in their stalls alongside about twenty Arab horses that were used in the Liberty act.

The Lipizzaners have a long and interesting history. They were bred in Spain originally, hence the name 'Spanish Riding School' but in 1580 Archduke Charles of Austria founded a stud at a place called Lipizza, in the Kurst Mountains above Trieste. He brought his foundation sires over from Spain and with extensive but selective breeding from his best mares the Lipizzaners were born. In those days horses engaged in battle needed extra powers of endurance, strong bone and muscle and most of all a bold but calm temperament – all traits found in the present day Lipizzaner. These characteristics, plus a noble carriage and presence, made him a natural choice for High School work.

Spanish Walk on 'Ziggy'

Having shown me the horses, Mrs. Vinicky went back to her wagon and I was free to wander round the circus on my own. It was much bigger than I expected. I walked between the lines of red living wagons, catching occasional glimpses of their interiors through the open doors. They all looked clean and inviting and families, dressed casually in jeans and sweaters, sat eating a meal or chatting together. It was difficult to associate these ordinary folk with the sequined and bespangled beings who flew through the air on a trapeze or made the children laugh with their red noses and baggy trousers. They were a cosmopolitan company. The performers came from Australia, America, Spain, Italy, France, Belgium, Czechoslovakia, Switzerland, Germany, Denmark, Austria, England – and now Cornwall! There were animals of all descriptions; horses, elephants, camels, Indian cows, zebras, llamas, lions, tigers, dogs, bears, monkeys, even a kangaroo. Some of them were not used in the ring but kept as zoo attractions. Passing the lions' cage , I saw a fine looking animal lying with his front paws protruding through the bars. He opened his mouth in a cavernous yawn, revealing long, wicked, white teeth. I wondered what sort of man the lion tamer would be. Walking on, I heard a noisy commotion coming from another cage. Two chimpanzees were having a fight. They screamed at each other in high pitched, almost human voices, jumping up and down like angry children. Later, Mrs. Vinicky told me they are very delicate animals and that in cold weather their cages are specially heated. The circus personnel seemed friendly enough but as I couldn't understand a word they were saying, all I could do was grin like an idiot!

The tent boys were still hammering away, disentangling ropes, putting up poles and gradually creating order out of chaos. The smooth running of the circus depends on the speed with which these men can erect the tents on arrival at the site, then at the end of the show, dismantle everything, pack it all away and have it ready to be erected yet again. Later, I asked Mrs. Vinicky how many men Cirkus Scott employed. She told me that apart from the performers who took no part in the manual labour, there were two hundred and eighty tent boys, electricians, wardrobe attendants, grooms, musicians and caterers. The running cost of the circus was in the region of a thousand pounds a day. I wondered how this assembly of men, women, children and animals moved from place to place and was told the circus took over an entire train of fifty two carriages. The ballet costumes alone needed four wagons. The Big Top was forty two metres in diameter and capable of seating a crowd of five thousand. Throughout the season, seventy five towns were visited. These facts and figures were staggering. Cirkus Scott's claim to be the largest in Sweden was no idle boast. The name 'Scott' seemed an odd one for a Swedish circus and it was explained that the directors, Kate Bronett and her son François were both Swedes, hence the spelling 'Cirkus' but they had been encouraged in the circus business by an English friend called Scott.

On that first night I sat in with the spectators to watch the show and get some idea of the general procedure. Mrs. Vinicky and Ulrika planned to do a double act for one night to give me a chance to get my bearings. The show was due to begin at eight o'clock and by half past seven there was a long queue outside the ticket office. Inside the living wagons there was a bustle of activity. Artistes were changing into their costumes and I caught glimpses of swift moving, sequined figures darting between the conglomeration of caravans and dressing wagons. Snatches of conversation could be heard in a variety of languages and to my joy I heard a group of young girls speaking English. It was a relief to understand what they were saying and when we had introduced ourselves they explained they were a dancing troupe from England. They were known as the Digger Pugh Girls and not only did several dance routines in the show but some of them also enhanced our High School Act by forming a tableau on the stage to give the horses an attractive backcloth.

It was fascinating to be able to watch all the 'behind the scenes' preparation. A clown, with white, deadpan face, sat on the steps of his wagon, practising his trumpet; a little dark skinned Arab boy, dressed in a sparkling scarlet outfit was doing cartwheels at an incredible speed. Occasionally I heard the roar of a lion and the more familiar sound of a horse neighing. Punctually, on the stroke of eight, the circus band played its opening fanfare and the chattering of the people died. The ringside lights dimmed and into the small sawdust ring came the Digger Pugh Girls, dressed in scarlet and black ringmaster attire. They entered via a stage which had been erected near the entrance to the Big Top. I was instantly impressed by their immaculate appearance, a spotless elegance which could probably be attributed to the competence of the wardrobe mistress. Their lively dance number was followed by comedy, provided by the Balconas, two Australians who did a slapstick performance on a revolving ladder. I was pleased to see two more English artistes, Reco the clown and his wife May, doing the same low wire balancing tricks I had seen them perform when they were with Bertram Mills. The Arab horses gave a spectacular Liberty display, their coats shining under the spotlights. They ended their show by waltzing to 'Tales from the Vienna Woods.'

The High School Act came just before the interval. The Digger Pugh Girls came on to the stage dressed in gold and white uniforms and carrying silver candelabra.

On Neapolitano with two little spectators

Having formed a tableau, they remained motionless throughout the performance. Mrs. Vinicky and Ulrika rode the same movements that would be required when I joined them; the ring seemed too small for the two horses so it was difficult to imagine how we were going to manage with three. Side by side, Neapolitano and Bellornato executed all the movements that Mrs. Vinicky and I had performed with our horses at Bristol; the Travers, Renvers, Spanish Walk, Passage, Polka, Pirouettes and the final bow in the centre of the ring. The spotlights emphasised the snowy whiteness of the horses' coats and the vivid colours of the riders' costumes. Mrs. Vinicky wore a long divided skirt of blue satin with a matching jacket, frilly white cravat at her throat and a blue top hat. Ulrika was similarly clad, but in maroon.

When they had completed their double act they left the ring but each returned to contribute a solo. Bellornato's was an unconventional turn on the forehand, where the animal's forelegs stay immobile while his hind legs do a circle round them until he is eventually standing with his front legs completely crossed – a hazardous operation, as the horse finds it difficult to keep his balance. Neapolitano's contribution was the Piaffe. He looked magnificent with a single spotlight highlighting his performance in the darkened arena,

After the interval it was the turn of the lions and tigers. They padded into the ring through the narrow tunnel with very wary expressions on their faces. I looked at my programme and saw that their trainer was a man called Herman Sontag. He was a surprisingly small man, but after a single, sharp crack of the whip, one could see he was in complete command. He was dressed in a crimson, military type of uniform. I was astonished to see he had brought two Dalmatians which he proceeded to tie to the bars of the cage. This was something I had never seen in any circus, although the dogs took no active part in the performance. Their very presence, however, emphasised the absolute control the man had over his animals. An even greater surprise was in store. As soon as the lions and tigers had assembled, a towering polar bear entered the ring and nonchalantly climbed on to a stool. The 'Big Cats' took no notice of him as he joined the performance. As I watched those lean, powerful beasts slinking round the arena, their paws leaving huge imprints in the sawdust, I marvelled at the subtle relationship between this man and his group of animals, who, if left alone, would have torn each other to shreds.

There has always been a lot of ignorant, ill-informed talk about cruelty in the circus. I have often heard people say, "I think it is dreadful to take wild animals out of the jungle and force them to perform tricks." It is a common fallacy to believe that these beasts are taken straight from the jungle. I would like to see any man force a tiger which had come straight from the jungle to jump through a hoop! No, the plain fact is that circus animals have either been captured when young or have been born in captivity. In either case, they have never known complete freedom and thus have never learned how to kill for food. Later, as I came to know Herman quite well, he told me a lot about their training. They are handled by man almost from the beginning of their lives and have learned to respect him. In some cases a bond of affection springs up between the trainer and his charges. Of course, the instinct to kill is never far below the surface and if a trainer oversteps the line which divides discipline from cruelty, the restraint, nurtured by long and patient handling, would undoubtedly snap and explode into snarling, clawing fury.

A few weeks later, I was to see an excellent example of this carefully instilled discipline. At one point in the performance the tiger was supposed to jump from one stool to another, over Herman's head and between his up stretched arms. The stool was knocked over as he jumped and the tiger tried to save himself by clawing at the trainer's bare head. A deep gash appeared and blood trickled down his head. The shocked silence of the spectators clearly conveyed their fear for his life. Herman, however, showed no trace of panic as the tiger managed to climb back on the stool; quietly, Herman turned to the other animals and completed the act while the blood congealed on his face. Immediately he was out of the ring, Herman was rushed to the hospital for stitches but with head bandaged, he was back in the ring again in time for the Finale. The confidence of that particular tiger, however, had been badly shaken and the following night he refused to jump. He was not forced to do so. The item was merely omitted from the programme.

The acts always followed one another in quick succession; clowns, acrobats, high-wire performers and various animals. Each act was first class in its genre. The evening ended with a parade of all the artistes. They walked down the steps from the stage into the ring where they formed themselves into a wheel, then marched round in time to the music, waving cheerfully to the crowd. The band always played the same tune for the Finale – 'I'm getting married in the morning' while the spectators clapped in rhythm with its jaunty beat. The role of the band in a circus is very important but not always appreciated. The timing must be perfect as it can make or mar a performance. Each act is accompanied by its own specially selected music. The artistes know exactly which act is in the ring, by the melody coming from the Big Top, even when they are sitting in their wagons.

Ulrika, me and
Mrs Vinicky in
Spanish costumes

The second morning we were up at seven o'clock to practise our triple High School. At first I went through the movements on my own. Mrs. Vinicky carefully explained each stage and I tried desperately to remember the correct signals or 'aids' as they are called. Ziggy was overfresh and much too eager to get into the following movement. I found it difficult to remember the sequence of each exercise and when the other two joined me, matters became even more complicated by Ziggy's determination to sink his teeth into Ulrika's knee as we rode side by side. For some reason he disliked having another horse too close to him and would spoil the desired effect of unity by laying back his ears and showing his teeth while the other two horses looked pictures of serenity. We went through the entire act three times, then someone else wanted to use the ring. My mind was in a turmoil as I still felt unsure of the details and I was supposed to be performing that evening. Mrs. Vinicky assured me that if necessary she would whisper the instructions during the actual show but I realised that with three horses working in such a confined space, it was essential for each rider to know her exact position – a collision would look most unprofessional.

By seven o'clock that evening my stomach was crawling with butterflies. Whenever I attempted to get the various movements of the act in their correct sequence, my mind would go blank. Make-up, too, presented a problem. I had never used grease paint, and as the strong spotlights drained my face of colour, a lavish amount had to be used. By the time I had finished accentuating my eyebrows and making my mouth into a scarlet gash, I looked more like a Red Indian than a High School Rider. The effect was so grotesque I had to wash it all off and start again. The costume I wore was similar in design to the others but not in colour. The long, flowing skirt was a soft pink, with a gold fitted jacket and gold top hat. Just as I was scrambling into it, Mr. Vinicky rushed into the caravan and said, "Hurry up, the act before yours is already in the ring!" I adjusted my spurs, gritted my teeth and felt I was being led to my execution. I could hear the clash of cymbals as the band heralded the feats of tumbling and balancing by the Italian Gimma Brothers. I think Ziggy sensed my nervousness as I climbed into the saddle. He danced with impatience and was taut with excitement. We rode towards the entrance and sat on our horses behind the heavy blue curtains. A volume of applause erupted and the Gimma Brothers came tumbling out of the ring. The moment of truth had arrived! I glanced up at the band leader who gave me an encouraging smile as he raised his baton. I felt the shudder that ran through Ziggy's body when he heard the soft rumble of drums that grew louder and louder until the crescendo ended in a clash of cymbals as the curtains parted, the house lights dimmed and we rode into the bright glare of the spotlights.

When I look back on that first performance, I still marvel at the fact that we got through without a disaster. One of the Digger Pugh Girls who had been in the tableau and had a clear view of the ring told me afterwards that she couldn't help smiling at the way Ziggy carried himself, declaring, "He looked like a 17 hh charger, with his head held high and his long, flowing tail streaming behind him like a banner." There was one moment when I thought there would be a calamity. Ziggy's solo contribution was to stand on his hind legs in the centre of the ring. He loved this part of the act and on this occasion he stood up so straight I thought he was going to go over backwards. He wavered for seconds before finding his balance and landing safely on all fours. At the conclusion of the performance we were supposed to dismount and acknowledge the applause. After first handing over our horses to the grooms we had to bow to the crowd and then back out of the ring until we were on the other side of the curtains. I found this to be the most alarming part of the whole act. Walking backwards in spurs is a precarious business and when one is encumbered with a long skirt, the operation becomes a nightmare; - and 'nightmare' is no exaggeration, for during the next few weeks I was plagued by a horrible, recurring dream. I would be making my elegant exit when the hem of my skirt would catch in my spurs and I would do a sickening backward somersault to howls of derision from the spectators. The end of the grand parade on that unforgettable first night, I quickly discovered, was by no means the end of the working day. The circus' two day stand was over and we were on the move once more to Vanna, a small town west of Umea.

As soon as the audience had departed, Cirkus Scott became a hive of methodical activity. First the tent boys went into action, hauling down everything they had so carefully erected; planks were piled on to wagons, cables disconnected and animals loaded into lorries for the trip to the railway station. We dashed back to our caravans, made a lightning change and with make-up still on our faces, ran to get the horses out before the tent came down around their ears. We then rode them to the station and loaded them into the waiting trucks. The saddles and show bridles had been carefully packed into boxes, so the horses wore old snaffle bridles and as they had already been rugged up for the night journey we sat on top of these, riding one horse and leading a second.

When moving, we sometimes rode as far as four miles to the train, which would be parked in a siding. Those rides were seldom without incident; Ziggy usually managed to cause some commotion. He hated standing still at the traffic lights and as we waited for the colour to change, he would rear up and paw the air

Bowing and backing out of the ring at the end of a performance.

My nightmare!

with his forelegs. The local children who habitually ran after us, crowded too close to the horses without understanding the dangers involved. Shouting at them in English made no impact, they just grinned and came closer. Some animals were transported to the train by lorry, others such as elephants and horses made the journey on foot. The elephants always led the way. They would leave the circus as soon as their act was over, ambling in their grave, ponderous gait, trunks holding the tail of the animal in front. This meant that they took much longer than the rest of the convoy. Quite often, one of the Gimma Brothers, whose act preceded ours, would ride with us, his strong baritone voice echoing through the night air as he sang his native Italian songs. At the station the horses were loaded into their box which they shared with two camels. The camels were at the back while the horses stood in two lines of three, facing each other, with a space in the middle for bales of hay, tack and sleeping quarters for the groom who always travelled with them. We took six High School stallions, some being substitutes in the event of any going lame. Ulrika and I sat with them until the groom, who had been helping to dismantle the stable tent, came to relieve us. The horses were not left alone for a moment, being stallions, there was always the danger that they might break loose and savage each other. When the groom arrived, we were free to return to our caravan and settle down to sleep while the train chugged its way into the night. During the first week with Cirkus Scott I found sleep almost impossible. Apart from the unfamiliar rumble of the train, there were weird animal noises, trumpeting of elephants, screams of quarrelsome chimps and roars of lions; sounds I had never heard on a Cornish farm.

After a while I began to get accustomed to the strange, nomadic way of life. Though it was theoretically a matter of routine and discipline, no two days were ever alike. As we travelled north towards Kiruna, the largest town in Lapland, there was little opportunity to admire the scenery but the names of the towns at which we stopped intrigued me; Skelleftea, Pitea and Lulkea, then over the border into the Arctic Circle to Mamberget and finally Kiruna itself. We were now truly in the land of the midnight sun. I shall never forget the eerie sensation of waking at three in the morning to find the sun streaming through the window. Outside it was as brilliant as an English summer's day. I must admit, though, my first reaction to the Arctic Circle was one of disappointment. I had imagined it would be snow covered with a clear, invigorating air. In reality, it was dusty on the unpaved roads and although there was snow on the distant hills, in Kiruna it was warm enough to walk around in thin cotton shirts. I watched the Laplanders coming into town from the outlying district on shopping expeditions. Some wore national costume. The men were dressed in navy tunics with heavy braiding across the shoulders and round the hem. Their baggy trousers were held up by thick leather belts which held long hunting knives, On their heads were knitted berets, with a cluster of red wool on the crown. The women wore red and navy shapeless dresses down to their ankles and bonnets tied under the chin.

I gradually began to make friends in the circus but though the other artistes were friendly, language difficulties prevented me from learning much about them as individuals. German was the most commonly spoken tongue and bursts of laughter usually greeted my attempts to copy their guttural voices. The tent boys vied with each other in trying to teach me outrageous sentences. I remember one lad who told me to say to his friend, "Sie haben ein gesecht vie ein affen." – "You have a face like a monkey." Circus life is, of course, not all spangles and sequins. The glamour and excitement of the sawdust ring is only part of the story – and to me, the least interesting. My greatest enjoyment came when the Big Top was deserted and early in the morning I would take a horse into the ring and practise alone. There, without the galaxy of staring eyes, I was able to relax. The silent rows of empty seats, divested of their nightly throng of indistinct faces, looked strangely stark and austere. Only the creak of leather or an occasional snort broke the silence. In that quiet atmosphere, both horse and I had a chance to iron out some of our difficulties.

The average circus spectator seldom understands or appreciates the amount of practising and hard work that goes into the production of a High School act. The less spectacular movements are often the most difficult to teach. Lamentably there are still people who insist that there is cruelty involved in teaching horses the Haute Ecole movements. In fact, some people think it is cruel to make animals do tricks at all. I think this is being over-sensitive. I am sure some animals, dogs in particular, really enjoy their circus work. The suggestion that horses are whipped to make them perform is ludicrous in the opinion of any true horseman. If a horse has been whipped, the resulting weals can not be disguised. No, the truth is very simple and undramatic. The essence of training any animal lies in two words, 'repetition' and 'reward.' Circus High School training is based on the natural movements that a horse will perform of his own free will. For instance, the Spanish Walk has been developed from the action of pawing the ground, which stallions in particular will use when confronted by a mare or another stallion. An excited horse will often execute the 'passage' of his own accord when first turned out into a field. To start teaching the Spanish Walk, the trainer must first induce the horse to lift a foreleg on command. This is done quite simply by tapping his leg lightly on the forearm.

The Digger Pugh girls on stage in the background

His natural reaction will be to paw, which is exactly what the trainer wants so he is patted and rewarded. Next he is taught to take a step forward and so on until from this simple beginning, the finished article is produced. The Liberty horses, too, are taught complicated movements which are gradually built up from something simple and easy for them to understand. I always used to think it was a miracle that they could find their own place in the line after being called into the centre where their numbers were deliberately muddled. Here again, it is 'repetition' that is responsible. Each horse is taught always to follow a certain stable mate until it becomes routine. In much the same way a domestic cow will find her own place in a long line of identical stalls.

One of my biggest problems during our High School performance was trying to keep a smile on my face. To Mrs. Vinicky it came naturally; she was a born artiste. Her bright smile endeared her to her audiences as soon as she entered the ring. Often she would turn to the people sitting in the most expensive seats, the boxes at the ring side, and give them a charming smile. They always showed their delight by their vigorous applause. I shall never forget the choreographer who came to the circus at Stockholm to rehearse a new routine with the Digger Pugh Girls. His English was very limited and he was trying hard to impress on them that they must smile more, especially at the people in the boxes. "Girrls", he said, "You must be more friendly to ze men in ze bushes!"

There are times, however, when the spectators are unaware that they are witnessing some feat of heroism, a time when the artiste has to force himself to keep a cheerful smile on his face. For instance, the night when Herr Sontag, calm and smiling, was commanding his tigers to jump through hoops and even over his head. Only the circus personnel knew that the animals had not eaten for some time. The organisation, for once, had broken down somewhere and there was no meat available. We watched with bated breath as the lions trotted sulkily into the ring and the tigers, with snarling, twisted faces jumped on to their stools. The spectators knew nothing of the tension and strain behind Herman's quiet smile, nor of the courage being displayed by a man who could walk into a cage full of hungry 'cats.'

Behind the scenes of any circus there is a fascinating tapestry of human drama; stories of gallantry and perseverance; happiness and tragedy. You learn to meet discomfort with humour, disaster with resolution. Community life is tightly knit; there is no escape from people. Privacy is little more than a word. If personalities clash, the reverberations are felt throughout the company. I speak from personal experience. The day to which I refer had been a chronicle of minor mishaps; nothing disastrous, but a steady stream of irritation. The High School practice in the morning had gone badly, the day was hot and humid with mosquitoes biting more viciously than usual. The last straw came about an hour before the start of the evening show. In the living room which I shared with Ulrika, our sole means of cooking was a somewhat temperamental primus. The thing seemed to possess a warped sense of humour. Sometimes it lit at the first flick of a match, at others, inevitably when we were late and minutes were precious, it became as stubborn as a mule. On occasions it pretended to light and just as we thought we had won, it would flare up in our faces. On this particular evening we were hungry so we decided to have our supper before the show began. Ulrika was doing everything she could to ignite it, including almost shaking it to pieces. I could see her temper mounting dangerously. I should have had enough sense to keep quiet. I made a silent bet with myself. Who would explode first? Ulrika or the primus? Suddenly a sheet of flame shot up to the ceiling, causing a black shower of soot. Unable to contain myself any longer, I burst out laughing. Ulrika turned on me in a flurry of fury. I'm ashamed to admit that the row that followed had little to do with the primus. It rapidly became Germany versus England!

When I returned to the caravan after the show, the place had been stripped of furniture and most of the utensils. Even the curtains had disappeared. Apparently they all belonged to Ulrika. She had left and moved in with some German girls. I noticed that the primus had gone too! I was pleased about that although I now had no means of cooking, nothing to sit on and no curtains to draw so that I could change out of my costume. I solved that problem by hanging my dressing gown over the window. The following day, Rosemarie, one of the Digger Pugh Girls came to join me in the caravan. This tall, fair haired girl from Kent changed the whole atmosphere. She had a wonderful sense of humour and a rare gift of being able to laugh in any predicament. I am glad to say it was infectious. All the girls rallied round and helped. One, for instance, gave us an old dress which Rosemarie ripped up and made into curtains. Mrs. Vinicky lent us some cutlery. We piled our suitcases together, threw a tablecloth over them, thus solving the table problem. One of the tent boys produced a second primus but its behaviour was nearly as unreliable as the first. Rosemarie and I bought our food jointly, putting an equal amount into the weekly food purse. It soon became a point of honour to see which one could wangle the most free gifts. The elephant trainer, who was a keen angler, kept us supplied with fish and often, on returning to the caravan we would find some kind soul had given us fresh fruit or other edibles. Our diet would have horrified a doctor. It consisted chiefly of cream cakes and coffee, with spaghetti as our main course because it was very cheap in Sweden. Rosemarie's

Rosmarie doing the splits (l) and in Mambo costume (r)

spot in the programme enabled her to nip into town during the show and be back in time for the Finale. She would bring a box stacked with cakes and pastries which the other girls had ordered. She became known as the 'Cirkus Scott Cream Cake Queen!'

On leaving Kiruna we headed south again, passing through wooded country towards Haparanda on the Finnish border. Most of the towns at which we stopped were small, only warranting one night stands which meant we had little time for sightseeing. We stayed for two days at Haparanda. It is a pleasant town at the head of the Gulf of Bothnia, which separates Sweden from Finland, so I had an opportunity to see a little of the Finnish countryside. Some of the other artistes walked over the bridge and explored the country on the opposite side. Amongst the circus personnel the language barrier did not seem to matter very much. Somehow we managed to understand each other but in the world outside the circus, especially in the more remote villages it became a more serious problem. One day this was brought home to me in no uncertain manner. First, I must explain that our groom, for reasons of his own had deserted the circus. This meant that Ulrika and I had to take turns sleeping in the train with the horses. It was a hair-raising experience. The only space available for the groom to sleep was between the two lines of horses. There was very little room and I would often wake in the night to find a mouth busily chewing hay a few inches from my ear. Sometimes a weird, high pitched croaking noise would come from one of the camels at the back of the truck. I could never get accustomed to that wail and it always frightened the daylights out of me. Looking back on it all, I often think of the danger involved during those night journeys. There was no communication between us and the train driver. If a stallion or a camel broke loose and caused a panic, there was no way in which we could have brought the train to a halt.

On the particular morning in which the language barrier became a problem, I had taken my turn in sleeping with the horses. Ulrika came to relieve me and we were told the train would be staying in the village for an hour. It was a remote place, somewhere north west of Stockholm so I took the opportunity of doing some sightseeing. A short while later, I returned to the station and was astounded to find that the circus train had gone! I had been left behind. I had no money and after a night in the horse box, I was dirty and dishevelled. Furthermore, I had no idea of the name of the town which was next on our circus schedule. In desperation I ran to a ticket collector and asked if he knew anything about the Cirkus Scott train and its destination. He stared blankly and shrugged his shoulders. There were some people waiting on the platform so I sought their help but with the same negative result. I might just as well have been speaking Chinese.

Soon another train pulled in and I eagerly scanned the faces of the passengers as they stepped on to the platform. I prayed I might see a face that at least looked English. Two girls came towards me but my heart sank when their blond hair and blue eyes clearly suggested Viking ancestry. They too looked completely blank at my enquiries,. I began to wonder what would happen at the circus when I failed to turn up. Would I get there in time for the evening performance? If only I knew where the circus had gone. After a while I felt like shaking the people who could not understand plain English, then I began to laugh at the absurdity of the situation. If I could not explain my predicament, I would be stuck on the platform for ever! At that moment I spotted a man in uniform and guessed he might be a railway inspector. I asked, "Do you speak English?" "A leetle," he replied. As far as I was concerned, a little was enough. Hastily I explained my problem. He told me not to worry and that he would find out where the train had gone. He came back a few minutes later with the details and gave me a free ticket to board another train. An hour later, I caught up with Cirkus Scott and amid cries of "Where on earth have you been?" I told my sorry tale.

We arrived in Stockholm on the first of August. It was a hot, sultry day and we paraded through the streets in full costume. We had been booked for six weeks and our schedule was a busy one. From Monday to Friday we had one show per day at eight pm; on Saturday there were two, one at 5 pm and the next at eight. On Sundays we had a very strenuous timetable with performances at two, five and eight. For the first few days it was so hot that the make-up melted on our faces and the horses emerged from the ring lathered in sweat. We played to full houses and I came to appreciate that the size of an audience influences the artistes. Rows of empty seats have a deadening effect whereas the expectant hush of a full house acts as a spur and intensifies the effort put in to a performance. It was in Stockholm that I learned something new about horses. I would never have believed that a horse could recognise a piece of music. On the opening night the bandmaster decided to have a complete change of tunes for our act. Instead of the clash of cymbals which normally heralded our entry to the ring, he chose a soft, lilting tune. Ziggy, who had always recognised the opening bars and became 'electrified', failed to respond to the new music. The other horses too, appeared to have lost the rhythm. Although we managed to get through the act, it took several performances before they became adjusted. One night an anonymous admirer sent each member of the High School Act a bunch of red roses. The flowers were presented in the ring, with a very flattering note attached. We never solved the mystery of the generous Sir Galahad.

After Stockholm we veered south again to Goteborg for a week and then on to Halsingborg for our final show. There was a sadness about that last performance. For four months I had shared in the lives of a colony of people of different colours, creeds and backgrounds. I had witnessed some of their trials and hardships, their fun and laughter too. Whether one was Arab, French, Italian, English, German or Spanish it made little difference. One was part of a team and colour or creed were forgotten in a common bond of friendship and loyalty to the circus. It was sad too to have to say goodbye to the horses, Ziggy in particular, with whom I had shared a most unusual adventure.

The Finale was like the last day of school. The artistes played practical jokes on one another and some of the cast swapped costumes for the parade. There was no breaking-up party as we had to take the horses to the station. They were going by rail across Denmark and then by ship to England. Our goodbyes were hurried, addresses were exchanged and many promises to write were made. I travelled home alone via Germany and Holland. In Germany I encountered a very different atmosphere from the one I had encountered in Sweden. Here the shopkeepers were brisk and efficient and welcomed you with a smile whereas the Swedes gave me the impression of being a bored nation – a nation whose high standard of living had, in some way, robbed the individual citizen of enthusiasm. After spending a few days in Bremen I caught the night train to the Hook of Holland.

In front of me now lies an old diary recalling those days. This is what I had written. "Arrived Harwich early morning - thick fog - ate hot sausages for breakfast on Paddington Station."

The adventure was over.

The grand finale

Reading the Cornishman in Kentucky

Chapter 8: **Across the Atlantic**

"America. Girl groom required for fabulous Blue Grass country of Kentucky. Three polo ponies-hunters. Able drive. Age in thirties. Modern stables. Passage advanced. Car. Excellent wages.

Write LOWRY WATKINS Esq., LONLEN, 5280 Orion Road, LOUISVILLE, KENTUCKY."

The advertisement in the 'Situations Vacant' column of 'Horse and Hound' seemed to flash across the page. I tried to ignore it but found myself turning back to it and re-reading the words. It was only six months since my return from Sweden and I had been surprised and a little disappointed at the lack of interest shown in my circus venture. To me it had been an extraordinary experience and I had imagined that people would have been eager to hear detailed descriptions of it but they seemed far more interested in what was on 'the telly.'

Perhaps it was this frame of mind that provoked me into replying to that advertisement. I heard nothing for several weeks and had almost forgotten about it when one morning I received a letter asking me to go to London for an interview. It explained that the Earl Fitzwilliam, a personal friend of Mr. Watkins, would be interviewing applicants on his behalf. Having heard nothing for so long, my original enthusiasm had begun to wane, especially as I knew no one in America and if I were lucky enough to get the job, I would have to travel alone. However, it was a challenge I could not ignore, so before I could change my mind, I caught the train to London.

The interview took place in Lord Fitzwilliam's office. I can't recollect the name of the street but I have a vivid memory of sitting on the edge of a hard, straight-backed chair, feeling like a schoolgirl who has been called in front of the headmistress. Facing me on the other side of the table, which was littered with papers, sat Lord Fitzwilliam, looking very much at ease. "How much experience have you had with horses? Can you drive a car? Could you take sole charge?" he fired the questions at me but with such charm that it was difficult to tell whether my answers were satisfactory or otherwise. He showed me some photographs of the Blue Grass country and of Mr. Watkins' stables. They looked very attractive. Suddenly I was extremely anxious for the interview to be a success. After a while the conversation switched to fox hunting. At that time, Lord Fitzwilliam was master of one of the oldest family packs of hounds in the country. The Fitzwilliam Hunt existed prior to 1760; records before that had been burned in a fire but since then the ownership of the hounds has never passed out of the Fitzwilliam family. When we said "Goodbye," I was given a reassuring smile as his lordship said, "Well, everything seems satisfactory. I will write to Lowry Watkins and tell him I think you are a suitable person for the job."

A fortnight later the job was mine. I was plunged into a whirlpool of form filling; visa applications, medical examinations and a visit to the American Embassy. There, I was obliged to spend a whole day and underwent such a thorough investigation that at the end I felt more like a criminal than someone merely applying to work in America. Nothing was left to chance – Reveal all, or else! Every birthmark, every scar was noted. I even had to declare that the scar on my stomach was nothing more sinister than the result of an appendix operation. I was shuffled from one room to another – one for a medical examination, another for my fingerprints to be taken, yet another for an interview. I was asked to declare this and to swear to that: "Why are you going to the United States? Have you arranged a job there? How long do you intend to stay? Are you going for an immoral purpose? Are you a Communist? Have you ever been one?" In fact – was my journey really necessary? The questions went on and on until at last they must have satisfied themselves that I intended neither to shoot the President nor set fire to the White House because, reluctantly it seemed to me, I was handed my visa.

I booked my passage on the Queen Mary which was due to sail on the 9th. June. David, a friend and neighbouring farmer, kindly offered to drive me to Southampton and we arrived early. As we walked on to the quayside and I saw the words 'Queen Mary' etched in bold black letters against her dazzling white hull, my mind flashed back eight years to the morning when Joan and I had stood gazing at the shabby little Maloja which was to take us across the world. Alongside this dignified, majestic Queen she would have looked like a comic court jester but she took us safely to Australia and I remembered her with affection.

The Queen Mary was due to sail at midday. We went aboard to locate my cabin and make a brief tour of the ship. Ignoring the rather curt notice, "First Class Passengers only," we took advantage of the general turmoil to explore the forbidden territory. The impression of abundant space and luxury was overwhelming. The gleam of polished mahogany, the reproductions of famous paintings hung on the panelled walls and the sparkle of silver gave us the impression of wandering into a stately home. I was quite relieved to return to the less opulent and homely atmosphere of the tourist class quarters. The 'all ashore bell' sounded. I thanked David for his help and said goodbye. As he walked down the gangway my last link with home disappeared. I was on my own. The tugs began to manoeuvre the massive ship away from the wharf and the few people watching our departure gradually became a blur as the span of water between ship and shore widened. We headed down Southampton Water. I took a deep breath. Another journey had begun.

The first day of any sea voyage always seems to follow the same pattern; passengers eye each other with a mixture of interest and suspicion. The young look for likely conquests; the older people congregate at the bars; the faint-hearted, determined to be seasick, wrap themselves in rugs, lie back in their deckchairs and prepare for the worst. Travelling alone can be a daunting experience but I was lucky. On the first evening I met a fellow countryman from Kent, called Bob. He was emigrating to America and had a job waiting for him in Virginia. – something to do with exporting grain. We became firm friends and found ourselves in a cheerful, cosmopolitan circle of young people. The five days passed all too quickly.

We reached New York on the 14th. June. I woke early, eager to catch my first glimpse of the celebrated New York skyline. I could see nothing but a grey mist. Gradually, as we edged nearer, the fog began to clear in the warmth of the sun and strange shapes appeared on the horizon. These curious apparitions soon became gigantic buildings, vast towers and spires, incredible skyscrapers, dark silhouettes against a sky which had turned a deep blue. Dominating them all was the Empire State Building which was easily identified by its long television aerial. We passed the Statue of Liberty, a tall, grey figure with her flame torch held aloft. We were close to the harbour now and as the Queen Mary made her way slowly towards her berth all passengers were called below where waiting officials inspected documents.

It seemed an interminable time before I was allowed to walk down the gangway and into the vast customs shed where mountains of luggage stood waiting to be claimed by passengers. People swarmed round these Everests of property like ants. I found my suitcases under the letter 'L'. There seemed to be very little organisation. The customs officials wore open necked shirts and no uniforms. It was difficult to distinguish them from the passengers as they intermingled with them. Eventually Bob and I emerged from the chaos of luggage, passports and certificates at noon – three hours after our arrival! My train for Louisville was due to leave Grand Central Station at four thirty so we decided to leave my luggage there. Bob's had been left at the docks for collection later.

We looked around for a taxi to take us to the station. A short distance away was a row of yellow cabs. The driver nearest to us chewed gum nonchalantly and spoke out of the corner of his mouth. "Where d'ya wanna go?" It sounded more like a threat than a question and I had an irresistible urge to snap back, "Wassit gotta do with you?" but instead I answered in an extra-polite voice, "Grand Central Station, please." – pointedly emphasising the 'please'. He drove very fast through a maze of back streets until we came out on to a very busy avenue.

Another yellow cab just missed us and our firebrand driver let forth a stream of invective in a broad Brooklyn accent. Suddenly I heard a noise which I had only associated with gangster films – the chilling wail of a police car siren. An enormous black car with a flashing red light on its roof raced past and disappeared into the traffic. I was thankful when we reached the station. The streets of New York, with traffic racing up and down on the 'wrong' side of the road seemed more like a set for a 'cops and robbers' film than real life.

At the station I made some enquiries about the train to Kentucky. "From which platform does it leave?" I asked. "Platform ma'm?" the ticket collector looked at me oddly. "It leaves from Track number five." I was already beginning to learn the American language. I had difficulty too in coping with the timetables. New York, for instance, was one hour ahead of Louisville and the clocks inside the railway station said something different from those outside.

Having only a few hours in which to see the city we decided to get a bird's eye view from the top of the Empire State Building. We found another yellow cab whose driver was a little more courteous than the first. He drove slowly through Manhattan, Central Park and Fifth Avenue. He pointed out the magnificent façade of St. Patrick's Cathedral, the leading Roman Catholic church in the country. In 34th. Street we reached our goal – one thousand , four hundred and seventy two feet high, with one hundred and two storeys of architectural genius growing into the heavens. The view from the Observatory stretches for forty miles to any point of the compass. From the top of the Empire State Building we could see the docks and the Queen Mary, which from that height looked like a tiny child's toy. Back at Grand Central Station again, it was time to leave for Louisville. I said goodbye to Bob and settled down for the twenty four hour journey that lay ahead of me. I began to wonder what the future had in store.

The train arrived in Louisville just before one o'clock on the following day. I had not slept at all and felt exhausted as I stepped out on to the platform in a blaze of sunshine. I saw a man walking towards me and recognised Mr. Watkins from the photograph which he had sent. He was a small man with a pale complexion and a severe expression. I guessed his age to be about sixty. He greeted me with a reserve which I later found rare among Americans. Having stacked my luggage into the back of an enormous green Chevrolet, we set off towards his home which was about fifteen miles from Louisville. Mr. Watkins began to describe his stables and outline my duties. He kept three polo ponies, two hunters and a pony which his teenage daughter rode at the summer shows. He also explained that he was divorced and that his home, called 'Lonlen' was run by a housekeeper called Mrs. Moser. We were driving through countryside which looked to be very English with a blend of trees and lush green fields. This was the fringe of the famous Blue Grass, home of the American thoroughbred, where some of the most prosperous stud farms in the world are situated.

Turning off the highway into a pretty country lane, I noticed its unusual name,

'Limekiln'. In front of us was a sub-division of attractive, one-storey houses, each with a neat, unfenced garden. Orion Road then led us to Mr. Watkins' home; a low, white-painted house which stood well back from the road and was the only one with a fence round the garden. Scarlet roses grew in profusion on either side of the path leading to the front door, which was opened by the housekeeper, Mrs. Moser. I liked her immediately. She had white hair, a gentle face with humorous eyes which seemed to be always smiling. She welcomed me warmly and showed me into the library where the walls were covered with pictures of horses and shelves stacked with books and various equestrian trophies. Mr. Watkins, having given orders that I should change immediately and meet him at the stables, disappeared to another part of the house. I thought Mrs. Moser looked sympathetic as she showed me to my quarters. I was being given no time to unpack or settle in. My 'quarters' turned out to be the guest house, a sweet little pine log cabin a few yards from the main house. It was built entirely of wood and consisted of a living room, bedroom, kitchenette and bathroom. It was comfortably furnished with a chintz covered settee, chairs, well stocked bookshelf and a coffee table. The bathroom was attractively painted in blue and contained both bath and shower. The house was air-conditioned and centrally heated; a fact which I appreciated later on in the bitter winter which was to come. From the tiny living room I could see a paddock sloping down to the stables which were partially hidden among the trees. Mrs. Moser pointed to a wooden carving of a fox which sat on top of the gatepost at the entrance to the stable yard. She explained it was by a a well known Kentucky sculptor.

Changing quickly, I found Mr. Watkins ready to show me the stables which he had designed himself and had mechanised to an incredible degree. Only four horses could be accommodated but each animal had its own loose box and sun parlour, the latter having wire mesh sides and concrete floors liberally covered with sawdust. In fine weather the horses could choose to live out in these or in the confines of the loose box. Each box had a drinking bowl which was thermostatically controlled, thereby preventing it from becoming frozen in winter. Feeding was done by an automatic time switch which allowed the oats to run down a chute and into the manger at the required times. The most unusual feature was the manure elevator. As the stables were in an urban area, a conventional manure heap was not allowed. Instead, it was taken straight from the boxes and put into an electrically driven elevator which in turn carries it to a covered cart standing outside. When full, the cart was towed away by tractor and sold to people for their gardens. There was also a vacuum cleaner for grooming, a fly killer and a fan – all electrically powered. Attached to the tack room was a small office with sink and hot and cold running water plus a telephone connected to the main house. I thought of the contrast of all this luxury and the circus in Sweden where the horses had been housed in tents and had to be content to share their quarters with the camels. Mr. Watkins showed me the polo ponies, Longa, Reina and Sombrero. The first two had been bought from Cecil Smith, one of the highest handicapped players in America. All three looked fit and hard.

Mr Watkins practising on the wooden horse

Having been given a general outline of my duties, I was taken to the practice arena where Mr. Watkins showed me a life-like wooden horse, which he proceeded to mount, then began practising hitting polo balls which I was asked to roll towards him. The sun was very hot and I was relieved when at last I was able to return to the cool haven of the little guest house to unpack and have a longed for cup of tea. Mrs. Moser had thoughtfully provided some immediate necessities in the way of groceries but I had to get the rest of the provisions from the shopping centre which was about two miles away. It was on that first trip to the super market that my story came almost to an abrupt and ghastly end.

Mr. Watkins had given me permission to drive his enormous Chevrolet, so after a cursory examination of the automatic gears which I had never seen before, I set off towards the highway. It was the first time I had ever driven on the right hand side of the road and the first time I had ever been on a four lane highway. Cars and trucks hurtled past at terrific speed and the Chevrolet lurched forward as I pressed too hard on the accelerator. I saw a sign 'To the Shopping Center'. Without thinking, began to drive towards it on the left hand side of the road! Suddenly I looked up to find a huge articulated lorry bearing down on me. I had been concentrating so hard on the unfamiliar controls of the car that I had veered to the left automatically. With a gasp of horror I wrenched desperately at the wheel and felt the rush of air as the lorry flew past. I caught a glimpse of the driver's ashen face as he just missed hitting me amidships. On reflection, I sometimes wonder how I survived those first few weeks. Getting used to American highways was not easy, especially when I had to tow a trailer behind the Chevrolet when taking the polo ponies to matches.

At Lonlen there were no set hours. Mr. Watkins frequently varied the pattern of the day, sometimes having polo practice very early in the morning, which meant getting up at 5.30 a.m. to drive the ponies to the polo field. At other times he would play in an evening match which necessitated in my working until after midnight. Mrs. Moser soon became a great friend and ally, helping me to adjust to the American way of life. We often had a good laugh at the mistakes I made in those early days. For instance, at the grocery stores I asked for a pound of biscuits and came out with some flat-looking buns – I should have asked for 'cookies.' One day I wanted some white cotton and was given a wad of cotton wool; I should have asked for white thread! I caused confusion too at the telephone exchange when I asked for 'trunks.' The girl thought I was slightly dotty until she established that it was 'long distance' that I wanted. Gradually I began to refer to petrol as 'gas,' the boot as the 'trunk' and the bonnet as the 'hood' so the garage attendants no longer looked perplexed.

Shortly after my arrival at Lonlen, Mr. Watkins departed on a business trip and Mrs. Moser went on her annual holiday. I was left in sole charge. I had not yet had time in which to get to know anyone and was still finding my way in new surroundings. On the first night alone in the house I lay awake listening to the crickets outside my bedroom window and from beyond the stables the tree frogs making their peculiar little noises. The scent of roses wafted through the mosquito netting and in the semi-darkness the tall trees in the garden assumed weird and menacing shapes. It was an eerie experience to be lying there completely alone in a strange country, not knowing anyone on whom I could call in an emergency. On the second night I was still awake at eleven o'clock when I heard heavy breathing. My stomach tightened into a knot and I felt the prickle of fear. There was a slight thud against the door. Had I locked it? I imagined a hand groping for the handle. Would anyone hear me if I screamed? The sound came again and I looked frantically round the shadowy room for something with which to defend myself. There was a long silence. I could picture the intruder creeping round the side of the house to look for another entrance. The waiting became unbearable, then I heard scratching and a low whine followed by a subdued little bark. Relief flooded through me as I got out of bed and opened the door. There on the doorstep sat a brown and white Spaniel with friendly brown eyes and a furiously wagging tail. I had had visions of a burglar and in my relief I wrapped my arms around the dog and brought her into the living room for the rest of the night. I later learned from Mrs. Moser that the dog's name was Kitty. She had belonged to the people who had owned Lonlen before Mr. Watkins, but showing a remarkable spirit of independence, she had refused to leave the place. From that night, Kitty hardly ever left my side. She came with me to the stables, followed me when I exercised the horses and slept in my house on an old rug. Whenever I was forced to leave her behind, she would always be sitting on the doorstep, waiting for my return and ready with a rapturous welcome.

During that lonely week I came to appreciate the companionship that a dog can provide. One night a thunderstorm erupted. It was more frightening than anything I had ever seen in England. The previous day had been hot, humid and very still but by evening the wind was beginning to rise. I heard the distant roll of thunder and as the night blackened the volume increased. Raindrops began to bespatter the rooftops and the wind increased to a raging gale. Piercing flashes of mauve lightning illuminated the sky and the thunder exploded directly overhead. It was as though a bomb had gone off and the whole house trembled. The trees swayed and creaked and at the height of the storm an electric cable was brought down

Kitty and I in the snow

and we were plunged into darkness. I sat with my arm around Kitty and felt a soft, cold nose pushing at my hand. She whimpered like a child needing reassurance and in comforting her, I lost my own fear. The storm raged on for hours but by morning its fury was spent. In its wake lay a trail of wreckage. There were floods in many parts of Kentucky and trees lay on the ground like dead warriors on a battlefield. Mr. Watkins returned to find that polo had been abandoned for a while. The fields were waterlogged and Goose Creek, a narrow, rock bedded river which I often crossed while exercising the ponies, had become a raging torrent.

Mr. Watkins decided to pay a visit to Lexington, the authentic heart of Blue Grass country and home of the American stud farms. He asked if I would like to go with him as it would give me the opportunity of seeing some of the most famous stud farms in the world. It was here that most of the Kentucky Derby winners were bred; horses such as Man o'War, Citation, Bull Lea and Nashua took their first wobbly steps on the lush green grass of the Calumet, Spendthrift and Claiborne farms. History is written in the very bones of this country. Located in north central Kentucky, the Blue Grass covers two thousand, four hundred square miles and has a reputation for fast horses, beautiful women and potent whisky. Sometimes the adjectives get a little mixed! But, is the grass really blue? In the spring the landscape is a rich green but local people will not accept this, they insist that the young grass has a blueish tinge. Could it be the reflection of those gloriously blue Kentucky skies?

On the afternoon that we visited Lexington the sun shone from a cloudless sky. Stretching away into the distance we could see mile upon mile of gleaming white fences. In the paddocks stood mares and foals, idly flicking their tails in the shade of enormous trees. Occasionally, in a fit of wanderlust, a foal would stray from its mother and suddenly finding itself alone, would gallop madly back, its whinnying upsetting the other mares who stood protectively beside their offspring. Turning into the driveway of the famous Calumet Stud Farm we passed a life-like statue of Bull Lea, one of the stallions bred on the farm, whose progeny have earned millions of dollars. At the top of the drive stood a white-timbered house with red shuttered windows and a pillared porch – typical of Kentucky architecture. Nearby, the horse barns, which are never referred to as stables in America, were also painted in red and white, the Calumet racing colours. As in most English racing establishments, the afternoon is a time of rest and the black stable lads were relaxing in the sun. I looked into one of the barns and found everything spotlessly clean and tidy. The loose boxes were spacious, with gleaming brass fittings. The name of each horse was inscribed on a wooden plaque above each door.

Leaving Calumet, we drove through country that would stir the heart of any horse lover; undulating hills with lush green grass rich in calcium and phosphorous that build bone and muscle. The white fences are repainted every year; looking down from the top of a hill, they resemble an intricate pattern of filigree lace. There were horses in every paddock, lovely thoroughbred mares whose bloodlines reached back into history; soft coated foals with baby eyes that tug at the heartstrings; lively spindle legged yearlings, and away on their own in double fenced corrals, were the stallions, some of them Kentucky Derby winners and some whose names had not yet been written on the scroll of fame. The Blue Grass is full of statues of famous racehorses, some of them almost lifesize. We saw the bronze statue of Man o' War, the most illustrious American stallion of all time. Throughout the region there are cemeteries for the horses which the Kentuckians have made their idols; some have elaborate headstones on the graves – such as the one commemorating Domino, known as 'the gentleman horse'. His epitaph reads, "Here lies the fleetest runner the American turf has ever known and one of the gamest and most generous of horses." Talking to some of the old grooms who had been with racehorses all their lives, one could detect the pride in their voices as they discussed their favourites. I shall never forget one weather beaten little ex-jockey who pointed to a mare and said, "When that mare drops a foal, it hits the ground running!"

When I arrived back at Lonlen I found Kitty sitting on the doorstep and her welcome was so rapturous I almost felt guilty for leaving her alone all day. Polo was resumed within a few days and I went to my first American match. It was played on a ground about fifteen miles from Lonlen and I took the two Argentine ponies, Longa and Reina in the Rice trailer towed by the Chevrolet. I was gradually becoming accustomed to the fast four lane highways and this time the journey passed without incident. When we arrived on the field I tried to find some shelter from the blazing sun but there were no trees and the heat was almost suffocating. Mr. Watkins played for the Louisville team whose captain, Warner Jones was a well known thoroughbred breeder. Between each chukka, which lasted for seven and a half minutes, the ponies came back to the lines in a lather of sweat and I was kept busy sponging, drying and walking them round to cool off. It was during one of the rest periods that I met an American journalist. He explained that he wrote for a Louisville magazine, 'The Courier Journal.' He said that it was the first time he had seen a girl looking after polo ponies and would like to ask me some questions. At that time there were very few girls working in stables in America and I had seen none on the polo field. The interview which followed is absolutely true and I can remember it almost word for word:

"What's yer name?"

"Laity – Ann."

"Lady Ann?"

"No! Not Lady Ann, Ann Laity."

"Waal I'll be doggoned."

"Why, what's wrong with it?"

"Nothing – jest seems one hell of a name."

He wrote my name on a pad and after putting a piece of chewing gum in his mouth he asked, "Where d'yer live at home?"

"Lands End."

"Is that a city?"

"No, just a few rocks."

"Waal I'll be doggoned. What's the name of your nearest city?"

By this time I was beginning to feel 'giggly' and answered in a muffled voice, "Penzance." I thought Penzance wouldn't mind being a city for one day.

"Penzzzzaaance," he drawled, "Spell it."

I spelt it slowly

."Oh, I know – tum te tum te ra te tum." His rendering of the Pirates of Penzance sounded more like an Indian war chant.

"Waal I'll be doggoned."

He then asked, "Is this the first time you've bin to a polo match?"

"No, I worked in a polo stable in Windsor Park, England."

"Who did yer work for there?"

"Captain Ferguson."

"What was he captain of?"

"The Life Guards."

"Oh yeah, a beach patrol!"

By this time I was almost in hysterics and found it difficult to explain the role of the Household Cavalry, but he hadn't finished.

"Have yer ever bin abroad before?"

I told him about Sweden and he said, "What were yer doing in a circus?"

"Riding a High School Horse."

"Yer mean that horses go to High School?"

"No, they don't go to it, they do it."

"They doo it? Yer must be kiddin'.

After explaining the intracacies of Haute Ecole, I'm not sure which one of us was the more bewildered but suddenly he thought of something else.

"How old is yer Dad?"

I told him I failed to see what that had to do with it, so he said, "Waal, how old are you?"

Just at this point the next chukka began and our conversation came to an abrupt end. A few weeks later an article appeared in the Louisville magazine, entitled, 'The groom's a woman.' I had to laugh all over again at my American interview!

It is easy to make friends in the States; their hospitality is such that it wasn't long before I was being invited to the homes of people whom I had only recently met. In Louisville there was an English girls' club where I was introduced to Marian O' Neil. She came from Kent and having married an American soldier at the age of nineteen, left home to live in Kentucky. She, her husband John and their two little boys lived about twelve miles from Lonlen. A few months later I was to have cause to bless our wonderful friendship. Marian had a lively sense of humour which was somehow very British and not at all American. There is a subtle difference between the two which is not easy to define. The British type is perhaps less obvious. I remember going with her one evening to see the British comedy 'Carry on, Nurse.' We were doubled up with laughter for most of the film but the American audience was unmoved by most of the jokes.

At the end of July I had another excursion into stud farm country, this time to the Keeneland Yearling sales which were held twice a year in Lexington. On my day off I was allowed the use of a little English Morris which Mrs. Moser and I shared. I drove once again through the legendary Blue Grass, where a poet once described the birth of a foal as "the arrival of a new soul in Paradise." The sales held at the Keeneland Racecourse are a great event in the lives of American racing men. Here, yearlings change hands for as much as a hundred thousand dollars. The sale ring itself is arranged like a spacious theatre, with the focal point a square of green sawdust enclosed by a single thread of white silk rope. The buyers sit on rows of red plush seats, sloping upwards on three sides while the auctioneer and his assistants, all dressed in dinner jackets, are seated on a raised platform at the side of the sale ring. The yearlings are led in through sliding mahogany doors by black stable boys wearing spotless white coats. American auctioneers are a law unto themselves, so when the bidding started I could not understand a single word. It sounded more like the tobacco auctioneers' chants than a man trying to sell a horse. As each yearling is led into the ring, a spotlight shines from the roof and accentuates an already shimmering coat, making a very ordinary animal look magnificent.

Towards the end of the polo season, Mr. Watkins played in some 'away' matches so we took the ponies to Cincinnati, Ohio, which is about a hundred miles north of Louisville. This gave me an opportunity of seeing more of the country, where a subtle change was taking place. The leaves were showing their first hint of gold and the grass was fading from a lush green to a dry brown. The hot, humid days when the temperature occasionally soared to 100° Fahrenheit, gave way to the cooler and more pleasant days of autumn. It was time to bring the hunters up from grass. I gradually roughed the polo ponies off and turned them out for a well earned rest.

Mr Watkins on 'Sombrero' about to play polo.

Although there was a pack of hounds which hunted around Lonlen, Mr. Watkins preferred to hunt with the Iroquois, a fashionable , more sophisticated pack whose centre was Lexington, about fifty miles away. He rode a good looking black mare of 16.2 hh called 'Fatal Step'. It would have done well in an English show ring. His other hunter, 'Welsh Tourist,' was to be my mount when I accompanied him. The Opening Meet   wasn't until November so in the meantime my days were filled with trimming, grooming and exercising.

One day in the middle of September while on a shopping expedition in Louisville, I saw large placards advertising the Kentucky State Fair. Mrs. Moser told me it was an event I ought to see as it was a kind of shop window for all the products and activities of Kentucky. A horse show ran concurrently with the Fair, which lasted for about a week. It was impossible to see everything in one day but I visited most of the main exhibition halls, one of which concerned the story of tobacco, Kentucky's chief product. It was intriguing to watch the various processes that a tobacco leaf has to undergo before it can be put into a cigarette. There were competitions of all descriptions from baton twirling to stock judging but it was the horse show, of course, that interested me most. All the breeds that originated in America were represented including Saddlebreds, Tennessee Walking Horses, Quarter Horses and Morgans. The American Saddlebred, though to me looks artificial, is a spectacular animal. There are two distinct types, the five - gaited and the three – gaited horses. Both carry their heads and tails in an exaggeratedly high position and both have a very high stepping action. The former, however, in addition to the three natural gaits of walk, trot and canter, are also required to perform two artificial ones, the rack and the slow gait. The rack is a very fast movement which looks like a trot but is executed in four beat time. The slow gait is a similar movement, but as its name implies, is appreciably slower. They are both shown in long-cheeked double bridles and the riders sit on the back of their saddles with long stirrup leathers, holding their reins high above the withers. In the five-gaited class, excitement runs high as the commentator gives the order, "Let them rack on." The horses, with long flowing manes and tails almost touching the ground, storm around the ring to the wild applause of the spectators.

The three-gaited horse always has a hogged mane and trimmed tail and is only asked to perform his natural paces, walk, trot and canter.

The Tennessee Walking Horses were fascinating to watch. They were originally bred from pacing mares, crossed with thoroughbred stallions and an infusion of Morgan and Saddlebred blood. Their paces are chiefly the Flat-footed Walk, which is the normal four beat walk and the Running Walk, still in four time but very fast and with a long, low, gliding stride. There is a saying in Kentucky that the rider of a good Walking Horse should be able to balance a full glass of whisky on his head without spilling a drop, such is the smooth precision of his going.

There were many other events of course, which are typically American. There were Barrel Racing, Cutting Horse classes and the Western Pleasure Event in which the riders wear expensive, colourful outfits and the horses are bedecked in silver-studded bridles and beautifully made Western saddles with silver fittings and engraved leather.

By the end of October the beauty of the landscape was breathtaking. I shall always treasure the memory of a Kentucky autumn. Every day I rode through the woods in the valley below Lonlen and the burning colours of the leaves with their vivid splashes of scarlet among the russets, bronze and gold were unforgettable. In the haunting silence of the trees the only sound was the swish of the horses' feet as they padded through the drifts of fallen leaves.

The Opening Meet was on the fifth of November and by the fourth the weather, always completely unpredictable in Kentucky, had changed dramatically. The temperature had dropped to freezing point and snow dusted the fields. Next morning, however, it had turned into a soft drizzle and Mr. Watkins, as unpredictable as the weather, I was beginning to learn, decided not to go. He suggested that I take the Morris and go on my own as a day off was due to me anyway. The Meet was to be held at Grimes Mill, not far from Lexington and the Headquarters of the Iroquois Hunt. I had already been told about the annual 'Blessing of the Hounds' ceremony, which was an ancient ritual held in honour of Hubert the Huntsman. Although many 'blessings' are held on the continent, the Iroquois is one of the few hunts in the United States which still carries out the medieval tradition.

When I arrived the hounds had assembled in front of an old ivy covered mill and I was astounded to see they were coupled together. The riders had all dismounted and were wandering in and out of the clubhouse, having just partaken of a lavish hunt breakfast. At a given signal, an Episcopal bishop, wearing robes of black, white and scarlet, stepped on to an old millstone and began the prayers. In one hand he held a prayer book and in the other a hunting staff. Even the horses seemed to sense the solemnity of the moment. They stood quietly as he blessed the assembly. It was certainly a unique ritual but I couldn't help feeling uneasy about the whole ceremony; it seemed wrong to bring the Church into something as controversial as foxhunting. The hounds were eventually uncoupled at one o'

Opening meet of the Iroquois Hounds and the Blessing Ceremony

clock and as the hunt moved off I noticed both horses and riders were impeccably turned out. By this time the drizzle had developed into a thick fog so as it would have been impossible to see anything, I decided to make my way home.

It is a matter of history that in November, 1960 Kennedy was elected President of the United States. History books, however, merely state facts. One has to live through the actual times to feel the atmosphere and emotions of the period concerned. I remember the election fever that ran through Kentucky at that time. It was a Republican stronghold and pictures of Nixon were plastered on every hoarding. Although the result meant very little to me I can recall sitting with Mrs. Moser until late into the night, watching the results coming through on the television screen.

It was just after the election that I had cause to be grateful for the friendship of the English girl. Things had not been going smoothly between Mr. Watkins and myself for some time. I found his rapid changes of mind impossible to work with and it was inevitable that one day I would lose my temper. I will not relate the details but the job had become intolerable and I told him in no uncertain terms that I was leaving. Before I had time to cool down I slung my clothes into a suitcase and stormed out of the house. When I rang Marian and explained what I had done, she generously offered to come and fetch me and told me I must come and stay with her until my plans were sorted out. On arriving at Marian's, faced with a crisis, true to English upbringing, the first thing I did was to sit down and have a cup of tea! Had I foreseen the awful frustration of the week that followed I would probably have gone straight back to Cornwall. At first I tried to get another job with horses. I rang all the local riding schools and scanned the horse magazines from cover to cover, all to no avail. Unemployment locally was depressingly high. The most promising reply was that someone would take me on in the spring. My money wouldn't last that long and I soon realised that a horse job was out of the question.

My original plan had been to work in Kentucky for twelve months and save enough money to enable me to see a little bit of America before returning home but the money I had saved in just five months would not have taken me very far. I was determined not to give up, however, and answered advertisements for shop assistants, waitresses and a variety of other jobs but as soon as they heard my English accent the answer was always no. There were too many Americans out of work for there to be any hope for me. I tramped the streets of Louisville for hours, haunting employment exchanges until I was weighed down with a sense of failure and depression. I could perhaps have got a job as a secretary but I had not learned to type. My funds were fast running out. I blessed Marian for her generosity but I could not impose on her for very much longer. At night I tossed and turned, unable to sleep. There seemed no way out. If only I had not lost my temper!

It was Marian who suggested a solution. At first I wouldn't even listen. I remember it was a Wednesday afternoon; the weather matched my spirits, dull and dreary. It poured with rain all day and I had returned from Louisville soaked to the skin. I had resolved to tell Marian that I would be leaving the following day and going back to England but she forestalled me by saying, "Why don't you call Mr. Watkins and apologise? Perhaps he'll take you back." I laughed at the idea; I felt my outburst had been more than justified and I couldn't face the ordeal of swallowing my pride to that extent. Nevertheless, her suggestion had planted a tiny seed of hope. I decided to ring Mrs. Moser to find out if anyone had taken my place. She told me that no one had come and Mr. Watkins was getting fed up looking after the horses on his own. Still, it wasn't easy. I couldn't bring myself to dial his number but the fact that no one had replaced me gave me courage. I rang him up. I said I was sorry I had lost my temper and that I would like to work for him again. There was a long pause and I wished I had not contacted him. He said eventually that he would think it over and I could ring him again in the morning. Inwardly I fumed. How typical of the man that he could not make up his mind. I would have to spend another sleepless night. The next morning I phoned without much hope but to my surprise and intense relief he agreed to take me back.

As I drove up the drive to Lonlen for the second time I could see Kitty sitting forlornly on the doorstep of the little guest house. When she saw me she came racing over and leapt straight into my arms. Her welcome, at least, was genuine. Mrs. Moser too, seemed happy to see me again and when I went down to the stables, everything was just the same as before. It felt good to have a secure job again and the chance to save enough money to travel round America.

Life in Lonlen soon settled down to the familiar routine. Although Mr. Watkins' behaviour was still aggravating, I learned to bite my tongue and we were studiously polite to each other. The hunting season was now in full swing but the weather was getting colder. I well remember my first outing with the Iroquois and my initiation to the unaccustomed ways of an American hunting field. The Meet was quite near Grimes Mill where I had watched the 'Blessing' ceremony. As we unloaded the horses the cold air hit us as if we had opened the door of a refrigerator. The hounds had already arrived and I noticed, as I had at the Opening Meet, that they were again coupled together. In all other respects it could have been an English hunting scene. There were about forty or fifty riders, well turned out; some were riding good looking thoroughbreds. As in England, a few of the men wore pink coats and top hats.

When the hounds were released I was surprised to see that they still wore their collars. To reach the first draw we had to cross a frozen creek and the ice crunched as the horses picked their way carefully along the river bed. The horse I was riding, Welsh Tourist, was about 15.2 hh and according to Mr. Watkins, was an excellent jumper. The country was hilly and the deep wooded ravines reminded me of the Devon and Somerset country, although later on we galloped across wide sweeps of rolling grassland. The Kentucky River, a tributary of the Ohio, runs right through the middle of Iroquois land. Hounds were put into a wood and from then on worked entirely on their own. The huntsman neither blew his horn nor encouraged them with his voice. It wasn't until they had left the wood that the hounds had any idea where he was. The first draw proved a blank and as we trotted along a lane towards the next, I had an opportunity to chat to some of the field. They were extremely friendly and ready to discuss horses and hunting. I asked how often they killed a fox and they laughed, saying, "We ain't killed a fox in years; they've got long legs out here and keep outrunnin' the hounds!"

At last the hounds picked up a line and for once the huntsman blew his horn. I looked round for someone to follow as I had no idea where to go and found myself behind the Master. Most of the fences are wire which means the country has to be 'panelled' with wooden constructions called 'chicken coops' that are built into every fence. These jumps, wide at the base and narrow at the top, are about three foot six inches. As there is only one place in each fence that can be jumped a queue soon forms. We had galloped across a large grass field and I saw the Master, followed by a whipper-in, jump one of these chicken coops but the person behind them refused, so I, thinking I was doing her a favour, sent my horse over to give her a lead. In fact, I was committing an American hunting faux pas. The lady in question happened to be the Master's wife and social etiquette demands that the more important members of the hunt jump first, lesser mortals following in their wake. Later in the day, Mr. Watkins informed me that I was a groom and that my place was at the back of the queue, not behind the Master! By 4.30 p.m. the field had dwindled and we started looking for the shortest way

Chicken coop

These are built into the wire fences of the Iroquois Hunt country

back to the horse box. I heard the huntsman blow 'Home' whereupon he trotted back to the kennels without attempting to find his hounds. They were scattered along the length and breadth of a valley and he casually told us that they would find their own way home in the morning. I wondered what would have happened to an English huntsman if he arrived back at kennels without his hounds.

By the beginning of December the temperature had dropped to twelve degrees below zero. Snow fell continuously; the path down to the stables disappeared beneath mounting drifts and I had to hack my way through to feed the horses. Exercising became a hazardous adventure; the snow camouflaged the frozen ponds and it was difficult to tell where they were. Although the freezing weather brought its problems, I hoped for a story book white Christmas.

I was not disappointed. When Christmas morning dawned, I looked out on to a white world straight from the pages of Fairyland. Icicles hung from the branches and when the sun came out, the snow glistened on every rooftop. In the trees, tiny scarlet birds about the size of a British robin, sat with puffed-out chest feathers. These were the Kentucky Cardinals, nature's own living decorations against the pure white background. Inside my little house I had made it very festive, with a Christmas tree and a lot of greenery. I hung a coloured photograph of the Queen beside a Westcountry calendar which showed a picture of Mousehole Harbour. There were photos of the family too and in spite of the miles that separated us, on this, my first Christmas away from home, they seemed very near. Later, when I telephoned them, their voices sounded as if they were in the next room. Marian invited me for Christmas dinner and we followed all the traditions of a British Christmas Day: the turkey, plum pudding, exchange of presents round the Christmas tree – it all made me feel very much at home.

January remained bitterly cold and on one or two mornings I had to warm the saddles before putting them on the horses' backs, otherwise they would cringe as the frozen leather touched them. The bits, too, felt like pieces of ice so I put them in hot water before placing them in the horses' mouths. When the thaw came it deceived everyone into thinking that the cold spell was over. I remember on one particular day I had driven over to Marian's for supper and there was no trace of snow. During the meal it suddenly grew dark, the temperature dropped to ten degrees below zero and within minutes there was a white world. People had warned me that this could happen in Kentucky but until then I had found it hard to believe. I was driving the small English Morris and when I started the journey back to Lonlen I was soon in trouble. Being light, the car had very little grip on the frozen snow and the wheels began to spin. The highway stretched in front of me like a ghostly white ribbon but it gradually became obliterated as the relentless, driving snow clung to the windscreen. I saw one car on its side with wheels still spinning and at another point a lorry had slewed sideways with its back wheels in a ditch. Gigantic trucks thundered past, their drivers apparently oblivious to the plight of the smaller motorists who might be in their way. The journey became a nightmare. The car slithered from side to side and at any minute I expected to be crushed beneath the wheels of some enormous lorry. I had driven about seven miles when without any warning the car gave a wheezy splutter and the engine died. I tried the starter but nothing happened. I was right in the path of the traffic but afraid to get out as the other drivers were determined to keep going. Snow speedily built up against the front of the car and I was now in a very dangerous position. I had to do something quickly. The traffic, in spite of the conditions, was going much too fast. I looked behind and for a few brief seconds there was a lull. Scrambling out, I managed to push the car into the side of the road. After the heated interior the cold air felt like a knife being slashed across my face. I was wearing high heeled shoes and as American houses always seemed to me to be over-heated, I was wearing a thin sweater. I have never known such cold. My feet had already gone numb and snowflakes were freezing into hard lumps on my hair. I knew it would be useless to try to stop a passing car so I looked – in vain- for any signs of habitation. There was a wide ditch by the side of the road and beyond that towered a wire fence. I began to have visions of freezing to death, when away in the distance I caught a glimpse of a lighted window. If only I could climb the fence I would be able to get help but by this time my fingers had lost all feeling. The ditch was too wide to jump so I had to squelch through the freezing mud. After a struggle I heaved myself to the top of the fence and fell into a pile of snow on the other side. The walk to the house, although only a few hundred yards, seemed to take an eternity. As a woman opened the door to my knock, I was relieved to see a telephone in the hall. I phoned Mr. Watkins who understandably, was none too pleased to be dragged out on such a night. It took him almost an hour to reach me – a journey that would normally have taken about ten minutes. He fixed a tow rope to the Morris and after another nightmare ride we arrived back at Lonlen where my frozen limbs came painfully to life in a hot bath.

In April the hunting season ended and Mr. Watkins informed me he would not be playing polo any more. I was given a month to find another job. This time I was lucky. I had heard through a friend that there was a girls' camp in New Mexico, run by a Mr. Rice who was advertising for a riding instructress. I wrote to him and received a prompt reply and good news. The references I had sent were apparently satisfactory and I could start on the first of June which was the beginning of the summer term. In the meantime I had received an invitation to stay with some friends in California and decided to visit them after the running of the Kentucky Derby which was to be held on the first Saturday in May and was an event which I could not miss.

I left Lonlen at the end of April. Although Mr. Watkins and I had had our differences we parted on friendly terms and I was sorry to have to say goodbye to Mrs. Moser who had been a staunch ally and a great friend throughout the time I had spent there. It was sad too, that I would never see Kitty again. The little dog had become my constant companion and I can still picture her sitting on the doorstep on the day I left.

Derby time in Kentucky is one of the main social events of the year. Huge house parties are held during the preceding week and the city of Louisville is gripped by Derby fever. Flags fly from every rooftop and massed bands parade the streets. The racetrack itself is at Churchill Downs on the outskirts of Louisville. It is named after the Churchill family from whom the land was bought by the founder of the Derby, Colonel M. Lewis Clark. The first race was held in 1875 and was won by a little bay horse called Aristides. However, it was due to the enthusiasm and hard work of a gentleman called Colonel Matt Winn, who, twenty seven years later, with a group of business men, bought the Downs for 40.000 dollars and devoted his entire energy to improving the facilities and making the Kentucky Derby one of the most famous races in the world. On the day before the race it rained heavily but Derby Day dawned bright and clear and by midday the temperature was in the eighties. I travelled out to the Downs by coach. The immense grandstands were already packed with eager race goers. Families spread their picnic lunches on the vast lawns while fountains played in the ornamental ponds which were surrounded by colourful flower beds. All-girl bands played throughout the afternoon. The girls were dressed like ice skaters in short, swirling skirts, they tossed their batons high into the air and caught them again with deft movements. Behind the stands the souvenir salesmen did a brisk business. The most popular commodity was mint julep in a glass with a racehorse pictured on the front. The drink was a mixture of bourbon whisky, sugar, mint and ice. It is an essential feature of the Derby, being a well known Kentucky beverage.

The whole scene was full of pageantry and colour but there were many differences between this meeting and our own great classic at Epsom. Here, there were no top hats, no morning coats and no exclusive enclosure. Dress was informal, with men in shirt sleeves and most women in casual attire. The race itself is run over a cinder track and not grass, as at Epsom. Both events are for three year olds but the English race is run over a mile and a half, the American one is two furlongs shorter. There are no bookies at the Kentucky Derby. All bets are laid at the Tote, with two dollars the minimum stake. I bought a race card and studied the list of runners. None of the names meant anything to me so I chose one at random. It was a horse called Sherluck, ridden by little Eddie Arcaro, one of the leading American jockeys. Placing my bet early, I managed to find a space on the rails beside two old men who were discussing the merits of previous Derby winners. The names rolled off their tongues in a typical southern drawl – Citation, Gallant Fox, Whirlaway, War Admiral, Swaps and many others who have raced themselves into sporting immortality.

Just before 4.15 p.m. a bugle sounded and the runners began to file past the stand. I was astonished to see that each horse was led by a coloured boy dressed in jeans and a brightly coloured shirt and mounted on a rough long haired pony. They looked incongruous beside the sleek, elegant thoroughbreds. The favourite was a little bay horse called Carry Back which had magnificent muscled quarters and a low, sweeping stride. Suddenly the noise and chatter of the crowd died as the massed bands played the opening bars of 'My old Kentucky Home.' People stood to attention and many an eye filled with tears as the song, beloved by every Kentuckian, touched a chord of sentiment in their hearts. Stephen Foster's song symbolises all the tradition and history of Kentucky and means almost as much to the true-born Kentuckian as the Star Spangled Banner itself. After the first few bars the whole assembly began to sing. I shall never forget the sound of a hundred thousand voices ringing out across the Downs, everyone charged with emotion.

There were fourteen runners and as they cantered down to the start I picked out Eddie Arcaro's colours; gold silks with a blue circle, red shoulder straps and a gold and blue cap. Starting stalls, though common in America, had not then appeared on English racecourses and I was impressed by the ease and speed with which the horses were lined up. After a few minutes a full throated roar burst from the crowd, "They're off!" The thrilling music of thundering hoofs grew louder and the field flashed past in a close-knit bunch. The jockeys' silks were an indecipherable blur and I looked in vain for Sherluck but the experienced eye of the commentator soon sorted them out. Globemaster was the first to break the line, followed by Crozier and Dearborn. The favourite's name was not mentioned until the half way marker was reached and coming into the straight in front of the stands, Crozier leapt ahead. It looked as if his powerful, devouring stride would carry him home into the Hall of Fame. Suddenly, however, a blue and silver figure, crouched on the back of a small bay horse began to flash his whip and his mount responded as though electrified. The crowd screamed his name, "It's Carry Back, the favourite." Only two lengths separated him from Crozier but the winning post was only a few yards away. Those who had backed him leapt up and down like Dervishes. Those few yards held the key to fortune or failure. Crozier, under intense pressure, drifted very slightly off course and as he did so, little Carry Back swept past him to win by three quarters of a length. I was so gripped by the excitement of the finish that I completely forgot about Sherluck until I heard the commentator announce that he had come fifth. At least he had given me a run for my money. Carry Back looked unperturbed as he walked to the winner's enclosure. His distended nostrils were the only sign that he had just galloped himself into history and as the customary garland of roses was placed around his neck, he looked as if he could have run for another mile and a half.

The faces of the punters reflected their emotions. Some dashed excitedly to the Tote, others looked sadly at their tickets and tore them slowly and deliberately into tiny bits which fluttered to the ground like confetti. For me, winning or losing didn't really matter, I was just thrilled to think that I had seen the famous Kentucky Derby. An American once wrote, "Until you go to Kentucky and with your own eyes behold the Derby, you ain't never been nowhere and you ain't never seen nothin'."

On that sun-drenched afternoon, I was inclined to agree.!

Chapter 9: **Journey westward**

On the morning after the Derby I began my long journey across America to California. I had arranged to meet Mr. Rice, the owner of the girls' camp where I would be working later in the summer at Amarillo in Texas. He had invited me to stay overnight with him and his family at their winter home so that we could discuss the job. From there I would travel on to North Hollywood to stay for a while with some family friends whom I had never met but who had originally come from Cornwall.

The Greyhound bus on which I embarked at Louisville was cool and comfortable and for a few extra cents one could add to one's comfort by hiring a cushion. It was interesting to observe the effect which different drivers had on the passengers, for, of course, on such a long journey they were constantly changing over. Some kept the whole party laughing and chatting as a result of their breezy repartee, others with less personality had a sobering effect, the passengers becoming silent and almost glum.

The first stop was Oklahoma City. Thinking of the long running musical, I expected to see cowboys striding along the main street but I was disappointed. Most American towns, to me anyway, have a dull sameness, with very few individual characteristics. One of the passengers however, did tell me some hair raising stories about the tornadoes which strike Oklahoma from time to time. Powerful whirlwinds have been known to lift a bus high into the air. Storm shelters are built beneath many of the houses as safety precautions. Farmers, on occasion, have emerged from their cellars to find that their buildings have been swept away and dead cattle found miles from their homesteads. We arrived late in the evening and I booked into a hotel close to the bus station. It was pouring with rain and as I walked into the welcome warmth of the foyer and paid my six dollars for a room, a morbid thought came into my mind. There I was, completely alone in a vast continent. Not one of my friends or acquaintances knew where I was that evening. If I died in my sleep, who would care?

By the next morning, my melancholy had vanished and we continued our journey, crossing the border into Texas. I had never before seen such an area of totally flat land. It stretched far into the distance on all sides – a bleak and dusty carpet of greyish brown, unmarked by either fence or road. Here and there, like spectres from science fiction, gaunt oil constructions stood eerily on the skyline. There seemed to be few cattle which were mostly Herefords and Black Polls.

 Mr. Rice and his family lived in Panhandle, the northern region of Texas, in a place called Borger which was about forty miles north of Amarillo, where we had arranged to meet. I had already received brochures of the camp in New Mexico so it was easy to recognise Mr. Rice from one of the photos I had seen. He was tall and slim and greeted me with a friendly smile which immediately put me at my ease. As we drove towards Borger he told me about his camp and the type of work involved. He owned a 110 acres in the Pecos River Valley, deep in the heart of the Sangre de Christo Mountains which towered seven thousand feet above sea level. The camp was only 35 miles from the old Indian town of Santa Fe, capital of New Mexico.

Mr. Rice explained there would be two five week terms for the girls whose ages ranged from eight to eighteen. The camp taught swimming, dancing, trampoline, nature study, archery, art, speech training, music, fencing, drama and riding. My job would be to teach both English and Western Riding and to be responsible for the twenty horses and ponies. Between eighty and a hundred girls attended each term and I would have classes of twelve to twenty pupils. Each lesson was of an hour's duration. It sounded as if I was going to be busy.

At Borger I found the America I had seen in cowboy films. Tall, bronzed men with creamy-white Stetsons perched on the back of their heads, strolled up and down the streets or chatted casually in small groups. They wore fancy cowboy boots, silver buckled belts and brightly coloured open neck shirts with knotted handkerchiefs round their necks. I almost expected them to be wearing guns at their hips. The scene was so like a Western film set. A teenage girl, wearing blue jeans and a large Stetson hanging down her back, rode by on a skewbald pony. I noticed it was unshod. Mr. Rice told me it was the regular practice in that region. Only ponies with exceptionally tender feet were shod.

At his house, a few miles from Borger, Mr. Rice introduced me to the rest of his family. His wife, Kitty, had been born in the Highlands of Scotland and had met him in England during the war. She was serving in the British Military Intelligence and Newcombe Rice was working in the American counterpart. Her twinkling blue eyes reflected a vivacious and friendly personality and she greeted me warmly in an attractive Scottish accent. Their daughter, Kathy, was about sixteen and their son, Scotty, a few years younger; both seemed very pleasant children.

That evening the Rices had some friends in for supper and I was introduced to the producer of a radio programme. I cannot remember the name but it was something like "People Behind the News." After we had chatted for a while, the producer, who was a woman, said that she had never met a girl groom before and asked if I would agree to be interviewed on her programme. She explained that it was a very informal show but it was with some trepidation that I went along to her studio in Borger the next morning. After a few preliminary questions over a cup of coffee she told me that the recording would be made then and there and would be broadcast that afternoon. A few weeks later the studio sent me a record of the interview as a souvenir. Not only was I unable to recognise my own voice, I was appalled at the number of times I had used the word "well" before answering the interviewer's questions. It was quite a lesson in "hearing ourselves as others hear us!"

The following day I set out for Flagstaff, Arizona, going across the parched, flat desert with only the weird shapes of the prickly cacti breaking the monotony of the landscape. Inside the air-conditioned coach it was cool and pleasant but when we stopped for coffee breaks and meals and stepped outside, the heat blasted into our faces like a blazing furnace. At first we passed gas stations, motels and stores but as we drove further into the desert, signs of human habitation vanished almost completely. At one stage the driver pointed to an apparently large lake of shimmering water just ahead of us but as we approached, it never seemed to get any nearer. It was like seeing a destination but never arriving. Suddenly the water vanished and only the dry desert remained. It had been a mirage, yet we had seen something incredibly real. I would have sworn that water lay ahead. By late afternoon we reached the Grand Canyon, glowing like fire in the rays of the setting sun. As I stood on the rim of this gigantic crater and watched the varying shades of rock strata change from crimson to copper and orange to brown as the sun sank lower, its magnificence defeated all powers of description.

The next morning I awoke shivering. I couldn't understand why until I looked out of the window to find yesterday's boiling desert covered in a mantle of snow. I blinked in astonishment. Was this some kind of nightmare? My fellow travellers were equally aghast and like me, had come unprepared for cold weather. Later, the bus driver, when turning on the heater, explained that these freak drops in temperature occasionally occurred in that part of the desert. After a few miles we emerged into brilliant sunshine again.

My friends in North Hollywood were not expecting me until the following week and in the meantime I had arranged to stay in Los Angeles with my mother's cousins, Austin and Gladys Purdy. We reached the city in the evening rush hour, just as everyone was leaving work. Thousands of cars, like scurrying ants met us as we entered the suburbs. Although I had never met Austin and Gladys and their large family, I was soon made to feel at home and almost immediately was whirled into a wonderful week of sightseeing and meeting their numerous friends. They took us to the famed Disneyland where all the fairy stories spring to life. We visited the Fairy Queen in her castle and shivered in the dungeons with the Giant's victim. We stepped ashore on Tom Sawyer's island. We travelled by canoe through a jungle swamp. One exciting episode was a ride in a miniature submarine, through mermaids' haunts to the depths of a lake. Not far from Disneyland is Knottsberry Farm, another favourite tourist attraction. It is a replica of an old Western town with realistic models of old-time saloon bars, gold prospectors and galloping stage coaches being attacked by Red Indians. The air is rent with the crack of gunshots and war-like whoops and cries.

One day we went into Mexico, south through San Diego and Tijuana, a small border town. Dark eyes watched us in every street and brown, skinny fingers clutched our arms, entreating us to buy gaudy souvenirs. Wide-brimmed Mexican hats hung in doorways and dust hovered in the hot sunshine. As I watched the men struggling to make a living from the tourists, for some reason it reminded me of the first two lines on the Statue of Liberty:

> Give me your tired, your poor,
> Your huddled masses yearning to breathe free ......

I thought to myself, how can a man breathe free when he has to beg a living from his fellow man?

From Los Angeles I went to North Hollywood, where I had been given the address of two Cornish exiles, Mrs. Cruse and her daughter Lynn. Immediately on meeting them I realised that their hearts were still buried deep in Cornish soil. Cornwall to them would always be home despite the fact that they had not been back for twenty years. During the war, Lynn had a tragic experience while working for the Red Cross. She was driving an ambulance in London during an air raid when it was blown up by a bomb. Thirty six hours later she was rescued from the debris, but had lost the sight of one eye. I admired her cheerful courage, for in spite of recurring bad health she always had a ready smile. The third member of the Cruse household was a large black Labrador dog called Skipper to whom the mother and daughter were absolutely devoted.

I wonder if everyone who visits Hollywood for the first time is a little disappointed. The name automatically conjures up a vision of glamour and glitter; of film stars walking along the streets; of palatial hotels and romantic night clubs. I looked in vain for any of these. At first sight, Hollywood is just another ordinary American town, with little evidence of the film industry. There were no screen celebrities strolling down the street but just occasionally one found traces of the famous. In a square in front of the well known Grauman's Chinese Theatre, for instance, there were labelled footprints of the cinema idols and in another street the stars had signed their names in the cement of the pavement.

Outside Hollywood, however, Lynn and Mrs. Cruse showed me the lovely San Fernando Valley and Beverly Hills, where the luxurious homes of film stars stud the slopes of the Santa Monica Mountains. We drove along Sunset Boulevard where you can buy a map from wayside vendors and find the exact location of each star's home. Aldous Huxley has called Beverly Hills "The city of Dreadful Joy." Outwardly calm and serene, with its palm-fringed streets and beautiful flowering shrubs and trees but at night police cars prowl and pedestrians are afraid to walk by themselves. The film stars' houses, though luxurious and expensive, are not homes but of necessity almost impenetrable prisons, ringed round by every security device available. Beverly Hills is reputed to have 1900 swimming pools, 1200 lawyers, 34 private detective agencies and 172 psychiatrists – a piece of information I found recently in an American magazine!

I shall always remember the warm hospitality and friendship that I received from Lynn and her mother. On the day before I was due to leave, something happened which brought for Lynn and me a few days of excitement that will live in our memories for a long time. It all started after we had paid a visit to the Hollywood Bowl, a huge amphitheatre shaped like a giant seashell, in which concerts and singing festivals are held. We were feeling worn out after all the sightseeing and decided to go back into town for a cup of coffee. On the way we passed the Moulin Rouge, one of Hollywood's biggest nightclubs. A queue was beginning to form outside, so being naturally curious, we asked a bystander what was happening. We were told it was the 'Queen for a Day' television show. It is one of the regular programmes on American screens and Lynn was about to explain it to me when she said, "why don't we join the queue and then you can discover what it's all about." An attendant came round and handed each person in the queue a card on which we were asked to write down any special wish and its particular promptings. The wish had to be a reasonable one which would be in the powers of the television company to grant. The cards would then be scrutinised by a panel of judges and the person whose request seemed most deserving would be appointed 'Queen for a Day' and her wish granted. I couldn't think of anything to write down which might warrant such an exalted title but Lynn was much more sensible about the whole thing. She wrote a brief summary of her unfortunate war experience and explained that as she was temporarily without a job, she would like a typewriter in order to do some home typing, thus earning some money. After filling in the cards we were ushered into the restaurant and drank coffee while the cards were being assessed. About a hundred people had entered the contest and it took so long for the result to be read out that Lynn and I were on the point of leaving when a man appeared on the stage and read out sixteen names from which the winner would be chosen. Lynn's name was among them and all the chosen ones were asked if they would kindly wait until the judges had selected four finalists who were to be invited to come up on the stage and read their own cards. The winner would be selected according to the strength of the audience applause. By this time Lynn was getting quite excited and when her name was included in the final four we could scarcely believe it. She went on the stage and a lovely corsage of roses was pinned to her dress. The finalists read their cards in turn, reminding the audience of the reasons behind their special wish. When Lynn had finished reading I clapped so hard my hands were stinging and I realised the rest of the audience were equally enthusiastic. After an interminable wait, the winner was announced – Lynn Rawlinson – her mother had married twice – she had been chosen 'Queen for a Day' and amid deafening cheers she was led to the 'throne', where a crown was placed on her head and a purple robe draped round her shoulders. The organisers explained that on the following day she would not only be taken on a grand tour of Hollywood, which was to include a visit to the MGM film studios, but she would also receive a typewriter, a watch, jewellery, a television set, four dozen roses, a dress and some furniture. The Max Factor beauty salon had also offered her a free make-up session and hair styling. I was delighted to learn that she would be allowed to take a friend on the trip round Hollywood.

Promptly at ten o'clock the next morning, a chauffeur driven Lincoln Continental with 'Queen for a Day' displayed in gold letters along the whole length of its side, arrived to pick us up. We were driven in state down the main street of Hollywood. People turned to stare as they caught sight of the familiar words. At the MGM studios we were given a conducted tour and then invited to watch part of the shooting of two films, "Mutiny on the Bounty" and 'The Four Horsemen of the Apocalypse.' In the former they were shooting a scene of the Bounty which was supposed to be battling against a very stormy sea. The 'sea' was a large pond being agitated by a wind machine and the ship was a model. When some months later I saw the film in a cinema, it was impossible to relate the finished product to the contrived scenes of Hollywood. After the tour of the studios we were taken to the famous Max Factor beauty salon where Lynn was presented with an elegant make-up case, a new hairstyle and finally she emerged with an immaculately made-up face.

At this point we were taken to lunch at one of Hollywood's best hotels – the Hotel Knickerbocker and in the early evening we were escorted to 'Ben Blue's Nightclub' in Santa Monica by an Englishman who worked for the 'Queen for a Day ' programme. Lynn was announced as the 'Royal Guest.' Hours later, we were driven home through the cool, starlit night. Our fairy tale had ended. We both sleepily agreed it had indeed been a day 'fit for a Queen!'

*Brush Ranch Camp
for girls,
New Mexico*

Chapter 10: **Brush Ranch**

The second leg of my journey was inevitably something of an anticlimax. As I travelled eastwards towards New Mexico I reflected on the incredible luck that had been mine recently, not only the television show and all the experiences that had followed but also the warm and generous hospitality that I had received from the Purdy family and from Lynn and her mother. Encountering genuine friendship when you are thousands of miles from home is something never forgotten.

My route this time went through Phoenix, Tucson and El Paso where I spent the night. The next day I walked over the border into the Mexican town of Juarez – a rough-looking town. I wandered round its hot, grimy streets, besieged by black-eyed Mexicans trying to sell me their wares, A flash of white teeth was the reward if you bought something but if you said "No" expressions became sullen and dark eyes glared with annoyance. I was very conscious of being white among so many swarthy skins and when dusk fell I hurried back over the bridge into Texas with a sense of relief.

The following day I reached Santa Fe, capital of New Mexico, where Mr. Rice had arranged to pick me up. Before ringing to let him know I had arrived, I spent a little while exploring the town. It is built on an old Indian Reservation and is a living monument to the past. Placid and unhurried, it has made few concessions to the 20th century. Indian families still sit cross legged on the pavements, selling their blankets, beads and brooches made from the local turquoise stone. Ancient churches and museums in the narrow, winding streets, look as if they have been there for centuries. Brush Ranch, the Rices' camp, was thirty five miles from Santa Fe. Mr. Rice picked me up in the late afternoon and drove carefully along the dry, dusty roads which gradually became narrower and more winding as we began to climb into the mountains. The scenery was breath-taking. Deep, wooded valleys threaded their way between high-peaked mountains, firs and pines, growing incredibly tall and straight, stood silhouetted against a sky suffused by the glow of the setting sun.

The Rice Camp was 7,600 feet above sea level on the banks of the Pecos River in the heart of the Sangre de Christo Mountains. I was still dazzled by the beauty of the landscape when Mr. Rice announced we had arrived. We crossed a wooden bridge over which an attractive archway was formed by large letters, also in wood, reading 'BRUSH RANCH'. On the other side of the arch stood a cluster of rustic cabins and beyond those I could see a riding ring and corral. I had arrived a few days ahead of the campers and instructors in order to get to know the horses and help with the general preparations. Each teacher had her own bedroom, meals were taken together in a staff dining room while the campers ate in a much larger room of their own. From my bedroom window I could see the Pecos River, its clear, sparkling water cutting a twisting trail through the soaring mountains. Although it was pleasantly hot during the day, the temperature dropped considerably at night and on that first evening we all sat round a roaring log fire and discussed the coming term.

The next morning, after a typical Brush Ranch breakfast of hot griddle cakes, with maple syrup, scrambled eggs, bacon, toast, red jelly and coffee, I was shown around the camp. The children's living quarters consisted of pine log cabins of varying sizes. Some had as many as six separate bedrooms. Each building contained a bathroom with hot and cold showers, bunk beds and wooden floors covered with brightly coloured Indian rugs. Nearby was a recreation hall in which children could play table tennis and have sing-songs round a piano. They could also sit in front of a blazing log fire, toasting marshmallows – a favourite pastime of American youngsters. Across the road from the hall was a blue tiled swimming pool. It gleamed invitingly in the sunlight but there was work to be done and no time to stand and stare.

The horses were enclosed in a large corral at the top of a short incline but when I reached it I was out of breath. I couldn't understand why until Mr. Rice explained the effect of the high altitude until you became acclimatised. At one end of the corral stood a spacious hay barn and at the other, a neatly kept tack room. Some of the horses were feeding from a long wooden trough and I was surprised to see little furry chipmunks darting in and out, snatching bits of food while the horses looked quite unconcerned. Mr. Rice told me a little of the characteristics of each animal and I tried to remember their names. As an instructor it is very important to match the right child to the right horse or pony. A highly strung child on an excitable pony could be a disastrous combination. He pointed to a nice-looking chestnut called Cheyenne and warned me that none of the children must be allowed to ride him as he was very nervous and apt to whip round suddenly when something frightened him. Later, I became very fond of Cheyenne and rode him on all the trail rides.

For the first few days I rode most of the twenty horses and ponies in turn, getting to know their names and attempting to assess their respective abilities. In a very short while I came to know the placid ones, the excitable types and the ones who could be expected to stand the most work. I can still remember the names of most of the ponies and their individual characters. For instance, the children's favourite was a grey, almost white pony with a kind, good natured temperament, called Beaver. He was always in demand. Then there was Old Chuck, the slow coach of the party, a chestnut with a blaze and four white socks; the ideal type for a nervous beginner. Only occasionally did his good manners lapse. When boredom overcame him he would decide to go back to the stable and there was absolutely nothing a small rider could do about it.

In addition to teaching the pupils, my duties included the feeding and general care of the horses and ponies. They were fed outside, with the fodder, pony nuts and a few oats, in long wooden troughs. Once again, their individual characters had to be studied. It was important to ensure that each animal received his fair share of food. The bullies had to be restrained and the shy feeders separated from the rest. Horses, like some humans, forget their manners when confronted by a feast. I soon found out that one particular horse was stealing food from the others, having gobbled up his own. Brownie, a lovely dark brown, with fat, sleek sides, would lay back his ears and commandeer the whole trough if I were not there to prevent him. In complete contrast, the little four year old thoroughbred, Peppy, who had racing blood in his veins, was the aristocrat among them and was much too polite to fight back. His lean ribs told their own sad story and I always had to find a quiet corner in which he could eat undisturbed. Within a very short time, he put on weight and was as fit as the others.

The other teachers arrived on the day before the camp officially opened. They seemed pleasant and easy to get along with, as like me, they had not taught at a camp school before. Betty, the Art teacher was a vivacious red-head from New Mexico. The swimming tutor was a young college graduate from Oklahoma, called Linda. Speech and Drama were in the capable hands of Miss Locke, one of the older members of staff. Mr. Rice himself taught dancing. He had trained at the School of American Ballet in New York and in the winter months ran his own School of Dancing in Texas. In addition to the teaching staff, there was a qualified nurse, a head counsellor and several senior counsellors. The latter were older girls whose responsibility it was to look after the younger children and deal with any problems that might arise.

Opening day was on a Sunday. All the staff congregated in the Recreation Hall to meet the children as they arrived. Some had come from as far away as New York and California. Their ages ranged from eight to eighteen. We quite expected some tears of homesickness. I did wonder what these American children would be like. The only ones I had ever seen had been on the cinema screen and their brash, precocious behaviour had not impressed me. However, these seemed polite and well mannered but with inbred Celtic caution, I decided to reserve judgment. I thought that when the strangeness of new surroundings had worn off it could be a different story.

Promptly at seven o'clock the next morning I heard a bell summoning everyone

Ready to go on a trail ride

out of bed. My first day had started. Before breakfast prayers were said on the banks of the river. As the American flag was slowly hoisted to the top of the mast the girls recited the Pledge of Allegiance with their right hands placed over their hearts. The bright morning sun shone on eager young faces as the words, familiar to every patriotic young American, rang out across the water ......

"I pledge allegiance to the flag of the United States of America, and to the Republic for which it stands, one nation under God, indivisible, with liberty and justice for all."

My first lesson began at 8.30 a.m., the pupils being the more advanced children who were supposed to have had previous riding experience. Earlier I had caught the ponies but left them unsaddled as saddling and bridling were to be part of the lesson. In the tack room a group of about a dozen girls waited apprehensively for the strange teacher from England who was going to make them ride on funny little English saddles. Most of the girls came from the Western states and had only ever ridden on heavy Western saddles. Much later, it was revealed that this particular class had been dreading our first lesson. Mr. Rice had mentioned the word 'dressage' and as they did not really know what it was all about, it terrified them. They had envisaged me as a martinet who would expect them to perform all sorts of tricks on unfamiliar horses. Knowing nothing of this at the time, I did wonder why they all looked so frightened when they saw me!

It wasn't long before they began to relax and I soon realised they were keen to learn about English horsemanship. First, though we had to learn each other's language, We found quickly that many differences existed in equestrian terms and some of my Cornish expressions had them hooting with laughter. I remember one little girl who giggled throughout an entire lesson because I said her pony was "like a cat in a gale of wind." And another, "as teasy as an owl." Americans often call a horse's fetlock "an ankle". This would be considered 'non-horsey' in England. When I referred to a chestnut, they would say 'sorrel', a piebald would be a 'pinto.' We constantly came across differences such as these which not only caused amusement but also made lessons a great deal of fun. As I got to know them I found that American children were not at all like those I had seen at the cinema. They were polite, willing to learn and generally speaking, being more extrovert than English youngsters, they showed their affection more readily.

As the term progressed it was interesting to note how the personality of each girl affected the behaviour of the pony she rode. For example, Peppy the thoroughbred went beautifully for a quiet child with sympathetic hands but if the rider was excitable or quick tempered, Peppy would fuss, break out in a sweat and become totally upset. Brownie, on the other hand, quickly took advantage of a timid child and went wherever inclination led him; yet in the hands of a more robust rider, he was one most industrious ponies of the whole bunch. This study of equine and human behaviour fascinated me. I found that both equines and humans responded to similar treatment; the nervous ones needed the encouragement of quiet words of praise while the more headstrong types required firmer handling.

As the children got to know the various qualities and idiosyncrasies of the horses the problems of assigning mounts became increasingly difficult. They all clamoured to ride the firm favourites such as the good tempered Beaver; the little bay, Pecos, whose good manners never lapsed; Prince and Joey, an inseparable pair of ponies, who never left each other's sides when turned out into the corral. Poor old Chuck, however, who was as honest as the day but whose main interest was his stomach, was scorned. It became a standing joke that any girl who misbehaved was given Chuck as her mount; from then on all her energy was harnessed to the task of getting him into a canter. I had five classes a day, three in the morning and two in the afternoon, each lasting about an hour. I tried to vary the lessons as much as possible, bringing in some light-hearted games as well as the serious business of learning to ride. Sometimes, by way of relaxation I took the children on trail rides high up into the mountains. The scenery was magnificent and the ponies climbed the narrow, twisting paths like mountain goats. The pure air was invigorating and I always felt awed by the sheer beauty of the pine trees which were as tall as church spires. Hundreds of feet below, the soft green of the Pecos Valley, with occasional glimpses of the river glistened in the sun like a silver thread. One of the rides, however, I shall remember for as long as I live. The thought of what might have happened still fills me with horror. On the day in question, I decided to try a new trail, one that I had never ridden on before. The class I was taking consisted of fourteen younger, inexperienced children. We started in mid-afternoon on a ride scheduled to last an hour. We were all in high spirits as the ponies picked their way carefully along the narrow, twisting tracks. I was riding Pecos, the reliable little bay. If I had been on the temperamental Cheyenne, the story might have had a very different ending.

As we climbed higher and higher the view became more and more spectacular but I noticed that the trees were shorter and rather stunted in the colder atmosphere and loose rocks were beginning to hinder our progress. The trail seemed to be leading us much too close to the edge and I was alarmed to see how precipitous

'Brownie' and I beside the River Pecos

the drop down to the valley had become. I decided it was time to turn for home. Only then did I realise, with slowly mounting horror, that the track had narrowed imperceptibly and it had become impossible for fourteen ponies to turn round simultaneously without the grave risk of slipping and hurtling over the edge. Recent rain had made the path slippery in places and in others it was beginning to crumble. I had no alternative but to ride on and hope the track would get wider a little further on. Five minutes passed and still there was no possibility of an 'about turn.' I felt my stomach tighten and my mouth become dry. I looked back at the children's faces and saw that the realisation of their dangerous predicament was slowly beginning to dawn. Some of them were inexperienced riders and if they panicked there would be a terrible disaster. The light was fading and as there is very little twilight in that part of the States, it would soon be dark. What could I do? To turn round was impossible. To go on meant risking the lives of both children and ponies. As I was deliberating, there was a sharp cry of fear and I saw a child sawing at her pony's mouth. The girl had looked down into the ravine and for a moment had been overcome by dread.

I had to do something quickly. I tried desperately to keep my voice calm and matter of fact as I instructed the children to dismount and lead their ponies for a few yards, telling them there would be a widening of the track a little further on. I prayed that it was the truth but inwardly wondered how the nightmare would end. A few minutes later, salvation was at hand. Around the next bend I noticed a huge boulder that seemed to hang, suspended over the ravine but as we came closer I could see that it was part of an outcrop of rock which gradually sloped down to the valley below. We led our ponies gingerly on to it and within a few nerve-racking minutes the whole party was heading for home.

I noticed some very white faces in the line but said nothing and to take their minds off the affair I asked them to teach me the words of 'America the Beautiful.' At first the voices sounded thin and faded but soon their words were ringing through the mountains:

"O beautiful for spacious skies
For amber waves of grain
For purple mountain majesties
Above the fruited plain
America! America!
God shed His grace on thee,
And crown thy good with brotherhood
From sea to shining sea."

Back in camp they heard us coming long before we clattered over the wooden bridge under the 'BRUSH RANCH' archway. It was an episode I shall never forget. It was entirely my own fault. The mountain trails around the camp were all perfectly safe but I should not have been on that one.

As the term progressed the girls were taken on a number of trips to Santa Fe. They attended the open air opera, toured the local art galleries and museums and browsed through the local gift shops. The instructors were given twenty four hours off each week, starting at five pm on Saturday and returning to duty on Sunday evening for a service which was conducted round the swimming pool. After this an award was made to 'The camper of the week,' the girl who, in the opinion of the instructors had shown the best qualities of leadership, industry, keenness and general helpfulness during the week.

On most evenings there was some form of entertainment. The drama teacher encouraged the children to put on shows of their own and the recreation hall rang with laughter as the older ones sometimes did skits on the teaching staff. Often we would sit round a blazing camp fire, grilling steaks and sausages, singing our national songs. There was great rivalry between the states; the girls from Oklahoma would try to drown the voices of the Texans with 'Oklahoma' versus, 'The yellow rose of Texas.' I taught the girls the words of 'God save the Queen' and they always insisted on singing it after 'The Star Spangled Banner.' A very happy spirit pervaded the camp and when difficulties arose they were tackled with cheerful determination. An example of this came towards the end of the first term. One night there was a frightening thunderstorm. The thunder reverberated through the mountains like the boom of cannon fire while the lightning flashed in brilliant streaks across the sky. Lashing rain whipped the tiny streams into frenzied torrents. At the time the children were in bed and the instructors had all assembled in the dining room for a nightcap. My first thought was for the horses; I suddenly realised that I had forgotten to open the corral gate which let them out into a large paddock where they used to spend the night. Opening the door of the dining room, I was just going to run up the hill towards the corral when a violent gush of water flooded into the room, bringing with it stones, mud and fragments of branches. In a few seconds the floor was inches deep in dark, dirty water and the debris floating into the kitchen. We froze in horror but the deepening water stung us into action and we raced for brooms, buckets and anything else at hand to stem the tide. Someone started to dig a trench outside in an effort to channel

Learning to fence!

the water away from the building. The rest of us, with jeans rolled up above our knees, waded through the icy water in our bare feet, trying to prevent the water from getting through to the rest of the house. Kitty Rice and I, the only Britons present, sang 'Rule Britannia' as we wrung the water from the sodden cloths into the buckets and burst out laughing when we realised how ridiculous we looked and sounded! As soon as the storm abated, I ran up the hill to the corral and was relieved to find the horses unharmed. The next morning I found a tree lying on its side in the paddock. If I had remembered to open the gate, the horses would almost certainly have been sheltering underneath it during the storm and some would probably have been killed.

Apart from the squirrels and chipmunks, I saw few wild animals in the mountains but one day a skunk hid under the floorboards of the dining hall. No one knew it was there until the most revolting smell pervaded the whole building. It was so bad that eating there became impossible so until it was killed we could not bear to go back to the dining room.

At the end of the five week term, instructors were expected to put on a show for the parents so that they could get an idea of what the children had learned. Every child was supposed to take part so as I had about forty five pupils it meant quite a lot of planning. I tried to put together a programme which would include everything we had done during the term and something which even the most inexperienced children could demonstrate. We started practising during the last fortnight and it meant a lot of hard work for both the horses and the girls. The highlight was going to be a Musical Ride by sixteen of the older children and the programme would include a demonstration of bareback riding; a comparison of English and Western riding; a demonstration by the younger girls of exercises on horseback; some gymkhana events and some jumping. Each instructor was also required to write a report on each pupil – a task in which I sometimes found honesty conflicting with benevolence!

On the evening before the last day of term, all the staff, children and helpers gathered on the banks of the river for a unique farewell ceremony. A short service was held and as we knelt in prayer, moonlight filtered through the trees and enveloped us in its soft radiance. The children became unusually quiet and as I watched their rapt faces, all the stillness of the evening seemed to be reflected in them. After the service, little candles were lit, placed carefully on pieces of wood which were then put into the gently flowing river. The flickering fleet danced and bobbed on the water and slowly disappeared into the darkness. No one spoke. There in the moonlit mountains we were filled with a sense of reverence and awe.

The next morning, all was hustle and bustle as everyone prepared for the demonstrations. The riding programme opened the proceedings and at ten o'clock the parents crowded round the ring. The music for the Musical Ride was provided by a record player which was discretely hidden in the Pump House from which I was able to both watch and change the records. The children wore white shirts, Stetsons and blue jeans and rode in Western saddles as we did not have enough English ones to go round. Luckily everything went as planned, even old Chuck rose splendidly to the occasion and actually cantered at the first time of asking. The bareback display by six of the best riders was heralded by a fast, spectacular gallop into the ring, the Post Horn Gallop providing the accompaniment. Changing into English saddles, the younger children then demonstrated all the exercises they had learned and the programme ended with gymkhana events and jumping. It had all gone without a disaster and by the parents' applause I knew my pupils had done me proud.

American children, as I have said, seemed to be more extrovert than the English and at the end of that last day of term I discovered how sentimental they could be. There were many tears as we said goodbye, though I suspect their sorrow was at parting with their favourite ponies. Many of them gave me presents and some have kept in touch ever since. By evening the camp was deserted and strangely silent. We only had a few hours to relax, however, for the next day another batch of campers arrived and we all took a deep breath and prepared for another five weeks of similar activity.

The second term followed much the same pattern as the first – different faces but the now familiar routine – and at the end of it all another farewell. I had made good friends at Brush Ranch and wondered if I would ever see any of them again. It was a wrench too, leaving the horses, especially Cheyenne whom I felt I was deserting. In the weeks that I had been riding him we had grown to understand each other and he had become almost placid but I knew his newly acquired confidence could so easily be shattered.

I had booked my passage home aboard the Queen Elizabeth, leaving from New York but first I had to travel back to Louisville to collect some luggage which I had left with Marion. The return journey from Santa Fe by Greyhound bus took me through Colorado Springs, St. Louis, Missouri and finally Louisville, where Marion and John generously gave me a farewell party. On the bus to New York I met a young American whose home town it happened to be so in the evening when we arrived he showed me around. In a few hectic hours I saw most of the famous landmarks; Times Square; Radio City; Fifth Avenue; Central Park and many others but I paid the price on the following day. In a daze of fatigue I leaned over the ship's rail and watched the outline of New York gradually disappearing into the distance. I was scarcely able to stay awake during the evening meal and as I climbed into my bunk was promptly seasick. To my surprise and disgust I was ill for the rest of the voyage and took little interest in either the ship or her passengers. When we reached Southampton eventually, those grey, drab looking docks were, for me, the gates of Paradise!

The crossing had indeed been a very rough one and to make matters worse, the ship had apparently lost her stabilisers. It was a great relief to walk on firm ground again and I was able to look forward to my first square meal for a week. My mother and sister had travelled up from Cornwall to meet me and as they waited for me to go through Customs I realised how deeply I had become absorbed in the daily life of another country. The clipped British accent of the Customs officials sounded strangely alien as I had become so accustomed to the casual American drawl. Their brisk, uniformed efficiency was quite different from the shirt-sleeved informality of the New York Customs officers. Commonplace characteristics of English life, which I had never noticed before, suddenly assumed a new significance. The cars, after the giant Buicks, Chevrolets and Thunderbirds of America, seemed to have shrunk and the policemen, minus gun and swinging baton, looked oddly defenceless. As we drove towards Cornwall, I was surprised by the greenness of the countryside. Visions of the great rolling plains of Texas and its harsh, brown landscape contrasted sharply with the neatly fenced English fields. The air, too, seemed softer. The September sun was gentle, unlike the raw, burning heat I had known in Kentucky. I noticed the flowered gardens in front of the houses, each with its own fence, dividing it from the next door neighbour. On the other side of the Atlantic one rarely saw a garden fence, a path or perhaps a row of flowers being accepted dividing lines.

We stopped at a wayside café for a cup of coffee and again the differences struck me as though I was the visitor. The coffee came accompanied by a jug of hot milk instead of the inevitable cream which one would get in the States - small, insignificant details in themselves, but symbolic of a different way of life. For a while it seemed strange to be driving on the left hand side of the road again and memories of that first, near-disastrous American drive came flooding back.

It was not until we drove through Penzance in the dark of the late evening and I caught a glimpse of the lighted windows in the castle on St. Michael's Mount that I felt I was really home at last. Was it Frank Sinatra who sang, "It's very nice to go travelling …. but it's oh so nice to come home!"

British polo ponies arriving in New York

Chapter 11: **Polo in America**

July, 1963

Two years had passed since my return from the States and I never dreamed that I would ever see it again. However, one day in late July I received a phone call that was to turn my ordinary routine summer into a unique adventure and an experience I shall never forget. The caller was Major Ferguson for whom I had worked in Windsor. Lord Cowdray is taking a polo team to America. Would you like to come and help with my ponies?" Before I had time to recover my breath he went on to explain that 14 ponies, 4 of them his, would be flown from London to New York in a freight plane. They would be accompanied by three girl grooms from the Cowdray Park Stables and three male grooms. From Kennedy Airport (then Idlewild) they would be transported by road to Milawaukee, Wisconsin where they were scheduled to stay for a fortnight and would then be taken to Chicago. They would be playing in international matches in both towns.

That was the bare outline that emerged from our conversation. The trip would last for about a month – and he wanted an answer as soon as possible." I gave it to him immediately, and suddenly, all the memories of my previous trip came flooding back. The flaming colour of a Kentucky wood; the thunder of hooves on Derby Day; moonlight on the mountains of New Mexico and Christmas morning in a fairytale landscape of pure white snow! The thought of seeing more of that vast continent was irresistible.

The ponies were due to leave on the seventh of August. We all assembled at the airport where loading was due to commence at 10 pm. It was a clear, moonlit evening. A cool breeze swept across the airfield as I waited for the horseboxes to arrive. I noticed two huge planes close to where I had been told to wait and wondered which of the flying giants was to be ours. A tiny Dutch freighter alongside them emphasised their colossal size. It was then that I caught sight of the polo sticks on top of a pile of luggage placed under the wing of the small plane. A horrifying thought occurred to me; surely this wasn't the freighter in which we were to transport 14 ponies, 8 people and a mountain of luggage across 3,000 miles of ocean? It looked incredibly small beside the other aircraft but my fears were confirmed when I saw the suitcases being loaded on board. The Cowdray Park ponies were the first to arrive. A steep ramp, boarded on each side, was placed against the door of the plane. I wondered what would happen if a pony refused to load and watched tensely as the first one was led quietly on to the ramp. He walked up and into the plane without hesitation and the others followed suit.

When my turn came to lead Major Ferguson's pony, Canario, on to the ramp, he was as obedient as the others and soon all were safely aboard. My first glimpse of the interior however, shattered any sense of satisfaction I had been feeling. The freighter was designed to take twelve ponies only. Extra room had to be found for two more. The padded stalls were arranged in pairs, each one bolted separately, with iron hoops across the top to prevent the animal from rearing. Behind the last pair of horses there was a small space, the only room available for the human cargo. By one in the morning the loading operation was completed. The luggage was stowed away and the ponies tied securely in their stalls. Everything seemed ready. Suddenly I heard a Cockney voice shouting, "Hey, Charlie, better give 'em some more petrol, It's gonna be rough up there tonight." I watched the faces of the other grooms and wondered if mine looked as pale as theirs. The ramp was wheeled away but the plane was still open on one side and I could see the small crowd that had gathered to see us off. They were standing, huddled together with tense, anxious expressions. None of the ponies had ever flown before so everyone was apprehensive as to how they would behave , Another reassuring remark came from one of the engineers." Eh, Fred, dont 'ee wind 'er up like that, she'll 'ave a 'ole in her soide. She cain't fly with a gert 'ole in 'er soide!"

At 1.30 a.m. the door was closed and we found ourselves abruptly severed from the outside world. The ponies began to sweat in the enclosed atmosphere and a fine mist of steam rose from underneath their rugs. The engines roared into life, reaching a crescendo as the plane became airborne. A groom stood at the head of each pair of ponies in case of panic. The two Dutch Airline employees then informed us they had been trained to use hypodermic needles and humane killers! A depressing thought.

Mercifully, none was needed. The only sign of fear was at the moment of take-off when the ponies neighed uneasily and pulled at their halter ropes, but as we levelled out and the noise of the engines decreased, they settled down to munch the hay that hung in nets in front of them. As the tension eased we had a chance, at last, to introduce ourselves. The other grooms were from the Cowdray Park Stables, three girls – Brenda, Bobby and Kit and two men – Fred and George. Major Ferguson's ponies were in the care of his stud groom, Mr. Cole and myself. Major Ferguson very sportingly travelled with us. The rest of the team followed by passenger plane. Having the two extra ponies aboard, there was very little room left for the human passengers so we stretched out on the straw in the tail of the plane and attempted to make ourselves comfortable. It had been arranged to have watches of two hours each so that there was always someone on duty to keep an eye on the horses. The steady droning of the engines soon lulled us into a state of semi-consciousness, so most of us were half asleep when quite suddenly the plane began to pitch and roll like a ship at sea. The ponies became frightened, so, abandoning all hope of further rest, we had to stand at their heads to try and calm them. We had run into a storm and I remembered the chilling words of the Cockney shouting, "It's gonna be rough up there tonight!"

The storm soon passed, however, and the blackness beyond the tiny, barred windows gave way to a dull grey. "We'll soon be over Nova Scotia," the pilot announced, "We're flying north of the normal passenger route to New York." The journey had taken 14 hours and we were all suffering from lack of sleep as we came in to land at Idlewild. It was 11.00 a.m., New York time and as the door of the plane was opened, I could see the heat haze shimmering on the tarmac and felt a blast of hot air. George Sherman, the President of the American Polo Association was there to meet us and we were immediately besieged by newspaper reporters, photographers and various officials. Apparently we had just made polo history, being the first team to fly the Atlantic. Journalists crowded round and as I had already discovered when in Kentucky, they were astonished to find that the grooms were girls.

American regulations regarding infectious diseases are strictly enforced and before each pony was allowed on the tarmac, its feet were immersed in a bath of disinfectant. We were also asked to wipe our shoes with disinfectant. Two hours later, after answering a barrage of questions, posing for photographs and filling in innumerable forms, we were allowed to go. Ahead of us lay a twelve hour journey to Milwaukee. The ponies and male grooms travelled by horsebox and the girls in an estate car. By the time we reached our destination we were hot, thirsty and very tired, so after making the ponies comfortable in the stables of the Milwaukee Polo Club, we were driven to a motel nearby and enjoyed the luxury of a shower and a real bed.

After a day's rest, the team arrived and serious practice began. The captain was Sinclair Hill, the hard-riding sheep farmer from Australia and at seven goals, the highest handicapped player in the team. He played in number three position. At number two was Paul Withers, a farmer's son from Sussex, rated at six goals. Lord Patrick Beresford at number one had a four goal ranking. Major Ferguson completed the team at number four, the back position, with a five goal handicap. The Marquis of Waterford, Lord Patrick's brother, travelled with the team as reserve. By this time I had got to know the other girls and found them all easy companions. We were given free use of a car and as the only one in the trio with a driving licence I was pretty busy.

The first game was played within a week of our arrival. It was the first leg of the Robert Uihlein International Cup, the trophy going to the team with the highest

The British Team l-r The Marquis of Waterford (reserve), Paul Withers, Major Ferguson, Mrs Anne Werner, Sinclair Hill, Lord Patrick Beresford

aggregate of goals from two matches. Our opponents on this occasion were Milwaukee, whose team consisted of some of the best players in the States: Their aggregate of twenty two goals matched the British team, which meant that both teams started on level terms.

The teams consisted of:

Britain: 1. P. Beresford (4), 2. P. Withers (6), 3. S. Hill (7) (Captain), 4. R. Ferguson (5).

U.S.:1. J. Kraml Jnr. (3,) 2. R. Beveridge (6), 3. G. Oliver (9), 4. R. Uihlein Jnr. (4).

In Polo, when teams with unequal handicaps meet, the handicap of each player in each team will be totalled. The lower total will then be subtracted from the higher and the resulting difference will be awarded to the team with the lower handicap. For example, a team with a handicap of twenty two goals, would receive three goals from a team with a twenty five goal rating. That is the general rule, but there are exceptions. Quite briefly, the mechanics of the game are fairly simple for the spectator to follow. The ground, boarded on either side, is three hundred yards long and one hundred and sixty yards wide. A team consists of four players; numbers one and two are forwards, three is a half- back and number four is the back. The game is controlled by two mounted umpires on opposite sides of the field. There is also a referee on the sidelines to whom the umpires may appeal in the event of a disagreement. Polo is an extremely fast game and can be very dangerous if rules are broken. It would take too long to relate the various infringements that can occur but very briefly, if a player does anything to increase the danger, he is penalised and either a free hit, or a goal is awarded to the non-offending side. When a player hits the ball and then gallops after it, he is said to be 'on the line of the ball;' he therefore has the sole right of way and one of the worst fouls is to cut across his path. The only legal means of forcing him to concede this right is by 'riding off.' An opposing player is allowed to ride his pony alongside and push the striker sideways by the weight of his pony only by leaning against his opponent. There is no off-side in polo; in fact, a good game depends on the ability of the players to interchange positions according to the pattern of the play. The game itself is divided into periods of seven and a half minutes; between these 'chukkas,' as they are called, there is a short pause which enables the players to change on to fresh ponies. If at the end of the game the scores are level, an extra chukka is played in which the first team to score wins the game, hence its title, 'sudden death.'

The sports columns of the American newspapers had been full of news about the British team. Headlines in the Milwaukee Journal read, "Polo history has been made today," followed by a description of our flight across the Atlantic. Television cameras had been following the team's progress since our arrival and over 6,000 people had gathered to watch the first match between Britain and America since before the war. Excitement and anticipation mounted as the commentator welcomed the players. The Union Jack and the Stars and Stripes fluttered high over the grandstand in the blazing sun as the two teams stood side by side for their national anthems. As the last notes faded, a great roar broke from the spectators. American polo enthusiasts have few inhibitions and 'root' for their teams with an abandon seldom encountered among British supporters.

Once the game had started we had little time to watch the play. Only the cheers and groans of the crowd gave us some indication as to what was happening on the field. We sponged down the sweating ponies, bandaged legs, checked stirrup leathers, sorted polo sticks and tended scratches and bruises, occasionally catching sight of an orange-shirted figure galloping towards the goal mouth, followed by a roar of, "It's a goal!" Then we knew that the British had scored again. Between chukkas, the spectators, some of them still clutching bottles of Schlitz beer, the famous Milwaukee brew, crowded round us, bombarding us all with questions. It was difficult to be polite and at the same time get on with our work. The publicity given to the 'limey girl grooms' had created a great deal of interest and speculation. The Americans found it hard to believe that a girl could be capable of looking after 'such a lot of spirited horses,' as one paper described them! While on the polo field, the girls wore a 'uniform' of lemon shirts and brick-coloured jeans; the male grooms were dressed in white shirts and dark trousers.

In this, the first game on American soil, the British team out-galloped and out-played their opponents to win by eleven goals to three and the spectators, despite their fierce patriotism, applauded our players with generous enthusiasm. It was a wonderful start to the tour but a few days later one of the ponies went down with a severe cough. We had read in the Press about a virus which had struck at the racing stables in Florida and started a coughing epidemic which was sweeping across equine America. By the end of the week, all our ponies had succumbed and exercising became a nightmare. We ruefully christened them 'the fourteen piece orchestra.' Each day they seemed to get worse, their oat ration had to be cut to the minimum and consequently they soon lost their high peak of fitness and

The British Team before a game

condition. It was heart-breaking for the team, especially after their brilliant first match.

The second leg of the Robert Uihlein International Cup was scheduled for the following week and the British players were forced to borrow American ponies. Having very little time in which to ride these unaccustomed mounts, they were narrowly beaten by eight goals to seven. Nevertheless, their previous victory gave them the higher aggregate of goals and at the close of the game the trophy was presented to the British captain. During our two weeks at Milwaukee both players and grooms were being interviewed constantly by newspaper reporters and magazine writers. One day we were all taken to the television studios and 'grilled' individually in front of the television cameras. That evening we sat and watched the programme – for me - a frightening experience I would not care to repeat. We also went to the Wisconsin State Fair, a huge agricultural show, run very much on the same lines as the Kentucky State Fair which I had seen three years before. By the end of the fortnight the horses' coughing had ceased but we travelled on to Chicago with heavy hearts for we had suffered yet another disaster. One of the Cowdray Park ponies had broken a leg during a game and had had to be destroyed. Bobby, who had been looking after the mare, was understandably heartbroken.

The polo stables at Oakbrook, Chicago, run by Paul Butler, are often referred to as ' the capital of the polo world.' There are twelve immaculately kept grounds and splendid stabling for several hundred horses. The wooden boxes are arranged in large squares with a grass plot in the centre of each area and a sand bath in which the ponies are encouraged to roll. Adjoining, is a practice arena made of peat and sand which is specially oiled to prevent the sand from blowing around. Near the stable yards there is a large restaurant for the grooms and polo personnel. The surrounding countryside is attractively wooded, with a winding creek adding to the picturesque setting. The Oakbrook Hounds have their kennels in the vicinity so we often heard them returning from cubbing. One morning while we were exercising the ponies the hounds found a fox and ran it right across the path in front of us. The heart-stirring sound of hounds in full cry had the ponies dancing on their toes and snatching at their bridles and as I watched the hunt disappearing over the horizon, the temptation to join them was almost irresistible!

The climax of the tour was to be the Butler National 25 goal Championship. If the British team could beat Tulsa, the reigning American champions, in this all-important match, then the £10,000 that Lord Cowdray had spent in order to send the ponies and personnel to America would be justified. September 8th. had been the date arranged but in spite of injections, cough medicine and devoted nursing by the grooms, some of the ponies were still not fit enough to play, so the decision was made to postpone the game for another week. Gradually, however, their condition improved and they began galloping again without signs of distress. Each one of us fussed around our own particular charges like mother hens but our devotion paid off, for by the following Sunday, not a single pony was coughing.

The match was due to begin at 2.50 pm. By lunch time all roads leading to Oakbrook were jammed with cars. Thousands of spectators swarmed across the field and among the cognoscenti, unflattering odds of ten to one were being laid against us as by now the papers had given detailed reports of the virus that had attacked our ponies. Quite unperturbed by the publicity and excitement that they had aroused, the ponies stood quietly in the lines, pricking their ears at the clicking cameras. It was a warm, autumnal afternoon and a few minutes before the match the booming voice of Jack Cartusciello, well known in America as 'The Voice of Polo,' rang out over the loudspeaker. He welcomed the British team and announced the Tulsa line-up. They were formidable opponents.

The team consisted of: 1. Tiger Romfh (6), 2. Ray Harrington (8),
3. Harold Barry (9) and 4. John Oxley (2)

Lord Patrick Beresford described his feelings as the match began, when writing later on in 'Horse and Hound' "...... a warning bell sounds and the players mount. It is a relief to ride away from the stomach-cramping, mouth-drying tension of the pony lines but there is still the long, slow parade and the playing of the National anthems. At last, back goes umpire Billy Meyer's arm and there is the familiar crunch as the line-up closes. The die is cast; the gates of fear have opened and shut; the game is on." Back in the pony lines we could hear Jack Cartusciello's vivid commentary, relating every incident. The first goal goes to the Americans, scored by the gigantic Harold Barry who at that time was reputed to weigh twenty stone. At the end of the first chukka the British team were 4-2 down and the ponies came back to the lines with flaring nostrils and necks that were white with sweat. The battle was fierce with no quarter being given on either side. By half-time the score stood at six goals each. The spectators cheered wildly at every goal scored, thrilled by the brilliant polo being played. Tulsa struck early in the second half. They were in the lead again. Our hearts sank. Then the excited voice of the commentator raised our hopes once more; Sinclair Hill had equalised. The tension was almost unbearable as the play veered dramatically, first one way, then the

Lord Patrick Beresford

other. The mighty Harold Barry scored two quick goals to put Tulsa ahead but his team's elation was short-lived. I caught a glimpse of Major Ferguson on Conga receiving a backhander from Paul Withers. An American tried desperately to ride him off but he saw only the glint of Conga's iron clad hooves as she raced away to give her rider a chance to score yet another goal. Tulsa, however, was still in the lead, and to quote once more from Lord Patrick's article " ...... we badly need a goal. Hill has sent me the ball and I am away alone, experiencing to the full that feeling so well described by Will H. Ogilvie":

> "What though 'twas more by luck than skill
> That gathered up the pass
> Before us lies an open goal and eighty yards of grass!
> Come all ye gods of Hurlingham,
> Come answer to my call,
> Give pace unto the twinkling feet
> That fly before them all."

Lord Patrick, riding his big white-faced mare Gussie's Love, certainly flew before them all and slammed the ball between the posts. At the start of the last chukka the score stood at ten goals apiece. The screaming spectators were on their feet; never again did they expect to witness such a game. This was inspired polo that would go down in history. But all the grooms were worried. If, at the end of the game, the score remained level, they would be obliged to play an extra chukka, the 'sudden death' decider. Would the ponies be fit enough to stand the extra strain that would be imposed on them? The enforced rest during the epidemic had taken the edge off the peak condition they had enjoyed. The minutes dragged by and still neither side could find an opening. The commentator announced that two more minutes of playing time remained. My heart went out to our gallant ponies who were fighting like lions – but would bravery be enough? "The hour bringeth the man," they say, but in polo it must bring the horse too. The ponies were very, very tired. Standing on the side line with Canario, ready saddled in case Major Ferguson wanted to change ponies, I had a clear view of the last minutes

Major Ferguson chatting to his stud groom Mr Cole and me

With Kit and Brenda in our 'uniforms'

of the game. I could see Paul Withers on Tambera racing along the boards when suddenly, almost faster than the eye could see, he sent the ball sizzling across the grass, straight between the posts. 11-10! Agonising seconds remained. That final bell just would not ring. Tulsa regained possession and for a moment looked certain to score but Lord Patrick swept the ball from under the feet of his opponent's pony, swerved as an attacker came towards him and the gorgeous 'Gussie' galloped as though all the hounds of hell were in pursuit, towards the American goal. The shot was good and then the blessed sound of the final bell rang sweetly in our ears. There was pandemonium in the pony lines; dripping sponges were flung into the air; we hugged the ponies; we hugged each other too. Wide grins of satisfaction creased the faces of the triumphant British quartet as they rode in. Major Ferguson, as was his custom, came round to give each of his ponies a lump of sugar. Bursting with pride, we rode our charges back to the stables. One must admit, that in sport, there are moments when the wine of success is sweet. This was such a moment.

Two days after the victory at Oakbrook we loaded the ponies into a horsebox and made the long journey back to New York. We all had the satisfying feeling of 'Mission accomplished.' Our departure from the airport, unlike our arrival, was a quiet affair. There were no crowds, no cameras, and no glare of publicity, for which we were very thankful. The flight was uneventful and at London Airport I watched the ponies unloaded and taken into their horseboxes to begin the journey to their respective homes. Sadly I saw them go and as the last box vanished from sight I turned to start my own journey back to Cornwall.

For me it had been an unforgettable experience – one more chapter to write up in my little red diary.

Orloff stallions and 'Troika' given to Mr Eaton by Nikita Khrushchev

Chapter 12: **America again**

As always, I was happy to be home again. It was September and the cliffs at Bosistow, with their carpet of heather and clumps of yellow gorse, had never looked more beautiful. The sea, the colour of wild bluebells, sparkled in the sunlight and the waves that had hurled themselves with impotent fury at the rocks during the winter, were now lazily caressing the pebbles on the beach at Nanjizal, the little cove adjoining our farm.

Whenever I came back from my travels it was always to these cliffs that I eagerly returned. I would ride across Bosistow Carn towards Porthgwarra, breathing in deep lungfuls of the fresh, clean salty breeze that drifts in from the Atlantic and watch the sea change colour with each varying mood. For me, the real soul of Cornwall lies, not in her towns, however steeped in history, but in the haunting cry of her seagulls, the crash of waves on her stark granite rocks and in the quiet peace of her lonely moors.

After my trip to America with the polo ponies I settled down on the farm quite contentedly for a while. I was soon involved in the familiar routine of hunting in winter, showing in summer and breaking in a few horses. This happy state of affairs lasted nearly four years, during which time I started to write this book but gave up in disgust as I felt my literary talents were sadly lacking. I read a lot, mostly travel books and autobiographies. One of the latter was a book by Mary Bosanquet called 'Canada Ride,' which made a great impression on me. It is an account of her ride on horseback across Canada from Vancouver to Nova Scotia. Her description of the country through which she rode, the people whom she met and the wild animals she encountered en route was so vivid that it reawakened my own yearnings for more travel and new experiences. I wanted to build a store of interesting memories which I could enjoy when I became too old to do more than just sit and remember!

One day in January, 1967, I was idly turning the pages of 'Horse and Hound' when I came across an advertisement which read, "Experienced girl wanted to work with show horses near Cleveland, U.S.A. Professional stable touring eastern States during season, etc., etc …" As I read it, I could not resist the temptation to write off for more details. A reply came within a week, explaining that Acadia Farm Stables were run by an English couple, Mr. and Mrs. Francis, who had been living in America for eight years. They were renting the premises from Cyrus Eaton, an 84 year old millionaire who was, apparently, one of the most colourful and controversial figures in the States; a capitalist who dared to be a friend of the Russians. Mr. and Mrs. Francis were professional trainers of show hunters and had an impressive record of wins at all the major shows including Madison Square Garden. Most of these horses were owned by wealthy clients who kept them at livery and had them schooled at the stable, but they themselves rode them at the shows. During an average show season, which lasts from March until November, Acadia horses might travel thousands of miles and stay away from home for as long as a month at a time. The young man who had been the head lad had been conscripted into the U.S. Army so a replacement was being sought.

I applied for the job and to my surprise received a prompt reply requesting me to attend an interview in Sussex which would be conducted by Mr. Frank Haydon, the expert in the Hackney world. I met him at his home in East Grinstead and he appeared to be satisfied. A fortnight later I had a letter from America confirming that the job was mine.

This time it was even more difficult to obtain a working visa than when I went to the States in 1960. After six months of form filling and letter writing, I eventually found myself standing in the booking hall at Heathrow Airport with the precious visa safely in my pocket. My difficulties, however, were not yet over. The TWA clerk looked perplexed as he examined my ticket. "I'm sorry," he said, " but this plane left ten minutes ago." "What on earth do you mean?" I replied, "The ticket says take-off time is 11 a.m. and it's only half past ten." He studied the ticket again and informed me that someone had stamped the wrong time on it. "So what am I supposed to do now? Walk?" He smiled feebly and began flicking through various timetables. The queue behind me was getting impatient and people starting to mutter irritably. After a while the clerk told me to go and look for someone else who might help. I found another official sitting at a desk with TWA written in large letters on a sign behind it.. I was in the middle of explaining my predicament when his telephone rang. He proceeded to carry on a lengthy conversation with someone called Cecil, completely ignoring my scowls. When it was over he turned back to me with a sigh and I was obliged to explain all over again how it had come about that I was walking around with a ticket for a plane that had already departed. I soon realised that he wasn't really listening – I think his mind was still on his conversation with Cecil – so I began to lose my temper. I demanded to see 'someone in authority' and was shown into the manager's office. Here, all was brisk efficiency. Within minutes I was sitting with a cup of coffee in my hand, a ticket for another plane and profuse apologies ringing in my ears. An hour later I was on my way.

As I roared up into the sky I thought of my feelings on the night we left for America with the polo ponies. I remembered that stomach-tightening moment when the plane door was slammed shut and the tension on everyone's face as we wondered if the restlessness of the ponies would turn into blind panic. This time, I settled back in a comfortable seat and waited for the stewardess to bring lunch.

The journey was smooth and pleasant and when I stepped off the plane at Cleveland I could see the heat haze shimmering on the tarmac.. Mr. Francis was unable to meet me until the following day and I was glad of the opportunity to rest in an air-conditioned hotel. The following morning he arrived in a smart red Buick. My first impression was of a quiet, courteous man in his late forties. He had a small moustache and a shiny, bald head. During the drive to the stables we chatted amicably about horses and many of the differences between American and English shows. He explained that in the States more emphasis is placed on performance than conformation and that every show horse is expected to jump. There were many other differences too, which I would learn as I went along. The Acadia Stables were about ten miles from the hotel where I had spent the night, just off the busy American Highway Route 8. We turned into a gravelled driveway between tall fir trees where a small white sign announced, 'Acadia Farms – Cyrus Eaton.' At the head of the drive which was bordered on each side with scarlet tulips and lilac bushes, stood Mr. Eaton's home, a white painted house built of wood with dark green shutters and an unmistakeable air of elegance. A neatly cut lawn sloped down to the stable buildings which were also painted white with dark green doors and windows, The yard was ablaze with colour. In the centre, surrounded by a riot of red and white geraniums, grew a tall fir tree and geraniums filled the window boxes which hung beneath every window. Scarlet roses climbed up the white fence encircling the riding ring which was just across from the stable. It was one of the prettiest yards I had ever seen.

Mrs. Francis had just finished giving a lesson and came towards us holding a tiny Jack Russell terrier in her arms. She looked quite young, with short, fair hair and blue eyes but when she introduced the terrier as 'darling Pimmy' in a rather high-pitched voice I somehow received the impression that she and I were not on the same wavelength! However, she was all charm and showed me to my apartment which was a delightful little flat nearby. It was beautifully furnished with oak panelled walls and it had every modern appliance in the attractive kitchen.

I changed quickly and went down to the stables to get acquainted with the horses which I had read in a magazine were 'among the top show hunters in the States.' The 'barn,' as stables are called in America, housed 18 horses, nine on each side, with enough space in the middle to serve as an indoor school. Outside each box hung a leather head-collar with a shiny brass tag attached, identifying the occupant. At one end stood the forage store, cleaning room and a tack room containing a large glass cabinet filled with silver trophies. I was shown the pride of the stables, a good looking chestnut horse who was only four years old but already stamped with the hallmark of a champion. His name was Metro Light, he had won the Canadian In-Hand Championship the previous year. He looked big and well, with a coat that shone with good health and hard grooming. Next to him was an attractive bay mare of about 16 hands high, called Girondole. She was later tried for the American Show Jumping team. Both of these horses were to be in my care and I could see I would have a high standard to maintain. Mr. Francis gave me a précis of the history and characteristics of the horses, then we walked across to another block of loose boxes which housed three stallions. Zagar, Vaterpad and Otlick were Orloffs, a breed of Russian horses. These particular animals had a fascinating background. It appeared that Mr. Eaton, the owner of Acadia Stables, had been a prominent figure on the American political scene. His shrewd business sense and varied interests, particularly in the mining of iron ore and the Chesapeake and Ohio Railway, eventually made him a millionaire. One of his most cherished dreams was to bring America and Russia closer together. His first move was to try to improve the trading of cattle between the two countries. He was a remarkable breeder of Shorthorns and soon persuaded the Russians to import some of his best stock. He became friendly with Krushchev and visited Russia several times to have talks with the political leaders and diminish the misunderstandings between the States and the U.S.S.R. As a result of his efforts, he was, of course, subjected to bitter criticism by the American public, even being labelled 'Commy Lover' by the Press – an ironic title for one of the biggest capitalists in the States! The Russians, however, appreciated Mr. Eaton's activities to such an extent that in 1958 the then Minister of Agriculture, Matskeritch, was commissioned to find a suitable gift for him. He chose a 'troika,' a type of Russian carriage, together with the three Orloff stallions. Later I was to see them hitched to the troika and giving rides to members of the Bolshoi Ballet Company when they paid a visit to Acadia Stables.

I soon found that Acadia was no place for the work-shy. Casual labour seemed to come and go. There was only one other permanent employee, a teenage boy called Bob. Mr. Francis helped out whenever he was there but most of his time was taken up with teaching pupils and schooling horses. I had arrived in June and the heat was utterly relentless. From the moment I got up in the morning until the sun sank behind the trees in a scarlet ball, there was no escape from it. Even in the comparative shade of the barn the thermometer read 90° F. and I grew accustomed to a constant trickle of perspiration running down my face as I groomed the horses.

My first taste of life on the American Show Circuit came exactly four days after my arrival. It started, for me, at two thirty in the morning, when I had to drag myself out of a warm bed to help prepare twelve horses for the 300 mile journey to Oxridge, Connecticut. Each horse had a light summer sheet; leg bandages over thick pads of cotton wool; a tail guard and a 'bonnet' fixed to the top of each headcollar to protect the poll. A vast mountain of equipment was required for twelve horses on a tour that was scheduled to last a month. Apart from saddles bridles, martingales etc., there were rugs, feed sacks, bales of hay, pitch forks,

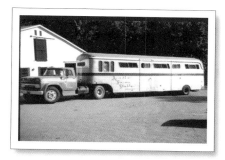

*Acadia Stables
10 horse lorry*

buckets, First Aid kits and a host of other things that had to be squeezed into an already bulging horse box. Somehow room had also to be found for suitcases, mackintoshes and boots which were very necessary in some of the thunderstorms which occasionally lashed the show fields.

Ten of the horses travelled in a huge articulated lorry driven by Mr. Francis. The remaining two horses were put into a Rice trailer and hitched to the Buick, driven by Mrs. Francis. I went in the car on this occasion and so had an opportunity of seeing some of the country. We drove through mile after mile of rolling farmland but it wasn't the countryside that I shall remember about this particular trip but a pathetic sight. We were driving slowly so there was time for it to be imprinted on my mind. At the side of one of the six lane highways I saw a big, shaggy, brown dog, standing guard over its dead companion which he would not leave. The dead dog lay at its feet. Presumably it had been killed by one of the speeding cars. There was nothing we could do. The pathos on that faithful dog's face haunted me for days.

The journey to Oxridge took 14 hours so I was already tired when we arrived at the show ground. The day's work had only just begun. Firstly, all the boxes allocated to Acadia Stables had to be located and the horses and equipment unloaded. After feeding, bedding down and making the horses comfortable, there came the mammoth task of sorting out all the gear and setting up the tack room. In America the temporary tack rooms are a unique feature of all the big shows. It had become the custom for the top professional stables to compete with each other in setting up the most elaborate model show rooms in which to display their trappings. At some shows a prize is awarded for the most decorative layout.

The Acadia Stable colours were green and gold, so first the partitions were covered with heavy linen drapes in those colours and a dark green carpet laid on the floor. Next, the highly polished saddles and bridles were hung around the walls, the bits and stirrups gleaming in the soft light of a pretty bedside lamp placed on a table in the corner. Photographs of horses adorned one wall and the colourful show rugs added a final touch of splendour. Across the entrance, 'ACADIA STABLES' was emblazoned in gold letters.

The settling-in process took several hours and by 12.30 a.m. I was more than ready for bed. As I was responsible for the well-being of the horses in the absence of Mr. and Mrs. Francis, who were lodged in a nearby motel, I was obliged to stay at the show ground. My sleeping quarters were at one end of the giant horse box, where I set up a camp bed. My washing facilities consisted of a bucket of cold water and a sponge. I think it was Touchstone in 'As You Like It' who said, "Home is a better place, but travellers must be content." I heartily agreed with him.

A life with horses is seldom one of luxury. They demand dedication, just like young children but I was hardly prepared for the immensity of work involved in travelling twelve horses round the country for a whole show season. That first show at Oxridge was a tough initiation to the hard work and responsibilities of life on the horse show circuit. It gave me a clear picture of the routine that was going to be repeated throughout the rest of the season. On the first morning we were up at the eye-rubbing hour of 4.30 a.m. As I gave the horses their breakfast I could hear the other grooms rallying each other with a commonly heard catchphrase, "Come on, you guys, shape up or ship out." Mr. Francis had engaged another girl to help Bob and me prepare the hunters for their respective classes. The Acadia horses were entered in almost every class so we had to work at tremendous speed. The majority of our clients were rich teenage girls who had no idea of the amount of work entailed in preparing a horse for the ring, in fact some of them did not even know how to put on a bridle as they had always been accustomed to having it done for them. However, one or two were first class riders and had won championships at Madison Square Garden. Most of the shows started at 8.30 a.m. Those that held evening classes under floodlights, went on until ten o'clock at night. We had no time for meals but snatched a hamburger or a quick drink whenever we had the opportunity. Every horse was turned out to a very high standard, with mane and tail plaited and hooves oiled. The standard tack was snaffle bridle and standing martingale.

The temperature often soared to a humid 95° F. at midday and by evening my head ached from the glare of the sun. It buzzed too, with unfamiliar words and phrases. I had to learn a new 'horsey' vocabulary which sounded very strange to English ears. I still laugh when I think of the girl who came galloping back to the stable and asked me to give her a bat. When she saw my perplexed look she explained that 'bat' is the American term for riding stick. I learned that horses are 'rubbed', not strapped; they win 'ribbons' not rosettes; schedules are 'prize lists' and loose boxes are 'stalls.' To confuse the issue still further, the classes are very different from ours. An Englishman, on picking up an American show catalogue would be mystified. He might read ……

Class 1. First Year Green Working Hunter
Class 2. Model Class
Class 3. Working Hunter Under Saddle
Class 4. Corinthian Hunter

Tack room set-up at major shows and sometimes entered into competition

It would take too long to define each of these terms. As a general rule, the emphasis is laid on performance rather than conformation in most of the classes. For example, the First Year Green is self explanatory. It is for horses competing in their first season at a recognised show. They would have to jump a maximum height of three feet six inches, whereas the second year horse would be required to jump three feet nine inches. The experienced Regular Working Hunters would have to jump four feet. They are judged solely on their style and accuracy over an outside course. A hunter should jump calmly, take off in stride at the correct distance from the fence, jump with arched neck and back and keep a regular, steady pace. The course usually consists of at least eight natural fences which may include a brush, in-and-out, wall, pen, chicken coop or aiken – the latter is a stiff post and rail with brush on either side. The Model Class Hunters are shown in hand and are judged as a led class would be in England, except that the animal can be any age. It was interesting to see that American judges never touch a horse while judging. They neither run a hand over his legs, look in his mouth, nor pick up a foot. I suppose they reckon that if they can't see it, it's not worth bothering about!

One of the most unusual classes was the Corinthian Hunter. It was open to amateur riders only. They have to be members of a recognised hunt and must ride in full hunting dress. They are judged - 60% performance, 25% conformation and 15% appointments – that is, the correctness of their attire. Every detail is checked; sandwiches must be placed in the cases; flasks must contain a beverage; spare gloves must be tucked under the saddle flap and stitched bridles must be worn as no studs or buckles are permitted.

The 'Working Hunter Under Saddle' has no counterpart in this country. The horse is judged entirely on his way of going, at the walk, trot, canter and gallop. Conformation is of no importance unless it affects his way of going. To an English judge, the American hunter's way of going would be considered sloppy, unbalanced and lacking any semblance of impulsion. They are ridden on a completely loose rein with a low, relaxed head carriage, rather in the same manner as the Western riders show their Quarter horses. This style of riding originated with the cowboys in the old trail riding days when a horse had to lower his head in order to pick his way along the rough mountain tracks.

Travelling the show circuit was rather like being with the circus. The outside world ceased to exist. News of current events trickled through occasionally but didn't seem to matter very much. There was no time to read newspapers nor listen to the radio. My day began at six a.m., sometimes earlier, and I was seldom in bed before midnight. The girl who had been engaged to help Bob and me stayed three days, then quit. She said she could not stand the pace at which we were required to work. Mr. Francis then hired a man. After only two days he swore, declaring, "To hell, with this goddamned work!" and found solace in a bottle of whisky.

We were often away from home for a month at a time, so it was bliss to return to the luxury of my apartment at Acadia for a few days of comparative peace, where I could revel in a hot bath and have regular meals. All too soon we would be off again, touring through Ohio, Illinois, Indiana, Pennsylvania, New York State, Connecticut, Massachusetts, New Jersey etc. By the end of the season I had travelled thousands of miles and survived many minor crises. Horses are the most unpredictable creatures. At almost every show at least one of them could be relied upon to do something completely out of character. For instance, a horse who would normally load without any trouble would suddenly refuse to go into the horse box; another would go lame unaccountably, just before an important class. I came to know a little of the idiosyncrasies of each one of them; Metro Light, for example, who always twirled his straw into a ball before he would lie down; Girandole, who refused to stay in a field on her own; and white-legged Desert Boots, who hated having his girth done up and once sank his teeth into my shoulder when I carelessly adjusted his rug one night.

As the weeks passed it grew hotter and more humid, with the mosquitoes biting with increased viciousness. One day at a show in New York State, we had a terrible thunderstorm. The whole showground was flooded and the stables were under water. They carried on with the classes and the horses came back covered in mud which all had to be cleaned off and the tack made immaculate before they were allowed to enter a following class. We were short staffed once again as yet another of our helpers had departed. I was dead tired and hungry, my feet ached and suddenly it occurred to me that Fate, or whatever it is that controls our destiny, was playing a game with me, observing just how much pressure I could take before I gave up or dropped dead. It was this thought that stirred my natural obstinacy and gave me the strength to carry on. My diary read ……

August 3rd. What a fool I am! Working like a slave when I could be at home in comfort. Dreadful storm today. Tack room under water, bandages, brushes etc., floating round in the flood. Horses filthy. Cleaning tack until midnight – only Bob and I left to cope.

The Pull Gate at Arcadia Farm. No need to bend down when opening the gate!

If I had not kept a diary I would probably have forgotten the discomforts and remembered only the many acts of kindness that also came my way. The gestures of generosity from complete strangers made it all seem worthwhile, after all. Among 'horse-people,' in whatever country, there is a special bond – a sympathetic understanding of each other's trials and problems which our beloved horses will inevitably thrust upon us. On the show circuit I encountered a camaraderie and friendship which often brought laughter into calamitous situations.

In September the season came to an end and with it a blessed respite from the stifling heat. Back at Acadia the sun had lost its ferocity and the glorious American 'Fall' lit the fires of autumn and brought magic to the countryside, setting it alight with colour. The maple trees flamed scarlet and then turned to pure gold. During our rides through the woods the horses padded softly through thick drifts of fallen leaves in a hundred shades of russet, bronze, orange and brown. The show horses were turned out for a well earned rest and I had time to do some instruction and ride the horses that came to be schooled. Edgar, the boy whose place I had taken, came back on leave from Vietnam and paid the stable a visit. He had left his old Ford car there and told me that when his leave was up he would give it to me as he was being sent back to Vietnam and would have no further use for it. Although it was old and rusty, in need of a few repairs, I was absolutely delighted, having no inkling then of the part it was going to play in my future.

'Metro Light' in the snow 1968

In November the snow came and the familiar landscape disappeared quietly and secretly beneath a dazzling white mantle. Well-trodden paths vanished overnight, leaving only the footprints of mysterious night prowlers. By Christmas the air had an Arctic bite and icicle stalactites, some five feet long, hung from the edges of the roofs. In the early morning the frost sparkled, even on the inside walls of the barn. Mr. and Mrs. Francis decided to go home to England for a three week holiday, leaving me in charge of the stable. They engaged another English girl, who had once been a Wren at Culdrose in Cornwall, to assist me. Kathryn Robb (Robby to her friends) had a dry sense of humour and we got on well together from the beginning. I now had time to get to know the local people. After the frantic rush of the show season it was very pleasant to be able to accept invitations to supper and spend quiet evenings at their homes. The Weil family were particularly kind to me. Their daughter Debbie often helped in the stable. I found a wonderful welcome too at the home of Raymond and Bernie Bourke, who were French Canadians. They and their six children, all of whom were grown up, showed me a friendliness which is a great comfort when you are far from home.

During that winter of 1967-1968 it snowed right up until March and perversely I began to long for the sun again. Although the countryside looked very lovely in its winter apparel, when you're struggling with frozen gate latches and burst water pipes with fingers rendered useless by the cold, your're apt to ignore beauty. During the show season and while Mr. and Mrs. Francis were in England, I had had very little time off, consequently by March I had accumulated a backlog of free time. I was given a fortnight's holiday and decided to take a trip to Canada. I travelled by Greyhound bus to Toronto, Ottawa, Montreal and Quebec. It was on the bus between Montreal and Quebec that an idea began to form in my mind. Edgar's gift of the car had set me thinking. For years I'd had a yearning to go to Alaska. There was something about the wild remoteness of the country that fascinated me. Now that I was the unexpected owner of a car, here was an opportunity – I could drive there!

When I returned from my holiday I told Mr. Francis that I would be leaving in June. The twelve months that I had initially agreed to stay would be up then. However, I knew that my savings would not permit me to stay very long in Alaska unless I could earn some money while I was there. Somehow, I had to find a job. It turned out to be easier than I dared hope. By chance, one day, I happened to be looking through a magazine and came across an advertisement of a riding school near Anchorage. It was called the Diamond H. Ranch and belonged to a couple named Taplin. I wrote and asked if they could give me a job and received a reply within a week. Mrs. Taplin explained that her husband and daughter did most of the instructing but if I would like to exercise and school the young horses, there was a vacancy. It was the ideal answer and I waited impatiently for June to arrive.

On May 4th. Dancer's Image won the Kentucky Derby but made history when he was subsequently disqualified for having Butazolidin in his blood, so the race was awarded to the second horse, Forward Pass. This time I had to be content to watch

*Mr Eaton and I
going for a ride*

the race on television but I could visualise the whole scene; the massed bands; the crowds; the singing of 'My Old Kentucky Home', everyone gripped by Derby fever.

June came at last in a blaze of sunshine. As I looked at the geraniums in the stable yard I remembered arriving at Arcadia and could scarcely believe that the year had come full circle. I had travelled many miles since then and seen the countryside in many different moods. On that first day it had been like looking at a blank page, now the whole place was alive with memories. I could picture the interiors of houses, knew the personalities of the people who lived in them, knew how the lanes and fields looked in winter and where the paths led.

On the morning of June 22nd, I was in a reflective mood as I packed the last of my belongings into the car and drove slowly out of the Acadia driveway, past the tulip beds and lilac bushes and Mr. Eaton's lovely home. I eased the car on to the busy highway and switched on the radio. Steve Lawrence was singing, 'What now, my love.' I smiled to myself at the aptness of the title – what now indeed? I had planned to drive north through Michigan to the Canadian border at Sault Ste. Marie and then follow the Trans Canadian Highway westwards to Calgary where I had been invited to stay with friends for the Calgary Stampede Week, then to go north through Edmonton to Dawson City and on to the Alaskan Highway. I tried not to think of the thousands of lonely miles which lay ahead of me as I drove away from Acadia towards Toledo, reluctant to leave familiar surroundings and people I knew. There was still a measure of security and some landmarks that I recognised. I drove past the drugstore with the friendly assistant who always greeted me with, "Hi, Limey;" the bakery where I used to buy delicious home-baked bread; the Post Office on the opposite side of the road where I mailed letters home; the library where I had spent many interesting hours among its wide range of books. American Highways are not ideal places in which to daydream, so I forced myself to concentrate on the road ahead. Huge truck-trailers would suddenly thunder past and I would have to hold on to the steering wheel to prevent the car from veering sideways in the 'whoosh' of wind.

My first setback came when I stopped for petrol at Flint, Michigan. The attendant, on glancing at my rear tyres, asked me how far I was going. "Alaska? You gotta be joking!" He soon convinced me that the tyres would not last another hundred miles, so with reluctance I parted with fifty seven dollars for a new pair. He also informed me that the radiator cap was cracked and that he didn't like the sound of my universal joint! Before he could depress me further with his gloomy forebodings, I bought a new cap and drove off. I now realised that the odd clunking noise to which I had grown accustomed every time I put the car in gear must have been the protestations of 'my universal joint.' Ignorance had been bliss but knowledge now gave it a more ominous sound. The counties gradually slipped behind me: Summit, Cuyahoga, Erie, Sandusky – strange sounding names. No doubt each had a fascinating history.

I reached Sault Ste. Marie, Michigan, commonly known as 'The Soo,' in the late afternoon. Facing this city across the St. Mary's River, on the Canadian side is another Sault Ste. Marie, the two cities being joined by the International Bridge, where I had to go through customs. There were few cars going through at the time and the customs official seemed eager for a chat.

"On holiday, Ma'am?"

"Yes, I'm on my way to Alaska."

"Alaska! But, you're not going to drive there alone?"

"I am if the car will get me there."

He looked at the old Ford in disbelief, at the places where the rust had eaten away the metal, at the pool of water already forming on the road beneath the radiator.

"What will happen if the car breaks down? Don't you know there are bears in Alaska?"

"Yes, but they tell me an Alaskan bear won't hurt you if you carry a stick – especially if you carry it fast enough!"

By the time I had cleared Customs it was getting dark so I decided to stay in Sault Ste. Marie for the night. From the outset I had planned to drive only during the day. Although the car had got me safely to Canada, my faith in its reliability was not very great and I did not want to risk breaking down in the dark. I found a reasonable hotel and that night I sat up in bed with a map of Canada spread in front of me. I looked at the vast continent and imagined, with a sense of incredulity, a little dot that was my car, crawling across the face of it.

The next morning I was in high spirits as the sun blazed from a cloudless sky. I set off northwards along the shore of Lake Superior, watching for the Maple Leaf sign and the figure 17 which indicates the Trans Canadian Highway. I had the road to myself, only meeting the occasional car as I drove slowly through endless miles of trees – tall pines and firs spearing into a blue canopy, giant maples whose branches fanned out overhead, obscuring the sun and turning the road into a dark and secret place invaded by weird shadows. At times I caught glimpses of the Lake, at others I seemed to be driving through a never-ending forest. In my diary I wrote ......'Hour after hour I drive and still there are trees, until it becomes difficult to believe that anything else exists.'

At intervals there were signs at the roadside saying, 'Antelope crossing' but I was never lucky enough to see one. I stopped for lunch at a remote little hamlet called White River which was reputed to be the coldest spot in Canada. In winter the temperature has been known to drop to 72° below zero. On a hot summer's day this was almost unbelievable. On and on I drove, through another afternoon of endless trees until I began to think I would never see an open space again. That night, however, I found a motel at Terrace Bay, an isolated little town right in the middle of the wild Canadian hunting country. Here it was easy to imagine wolves howling in the night and cries of coyotes as they slunk through the trees on their nocturnal prowls.

Before I left Cleveland I had worked out a rough budget as to how much I could afford to spend per day. In order to save money on food I bought loaves of bread, butter, fresh fruit etc. and stored them in an ice box that the Weil family had given me when I left. I found it invaluable in the hot climate. At Fort William I crossed into another time zone, from Eastern to Central Time and was obliged to put my watch back an hour. I had by this time driven almost a thousand miles despite the dire warnings of every garage attendant whenever I stopped for petrol. The universal joint was miraculously intact although the 'clunk' was noticeably louder and I found I had to stop more often to allow the engine to cool off.

At long last the forest became less dense and the country began to open out as I drove into Dryden, my last stop before Winnipeg. The only distinctive feature that I remember about this town is that there was an enormous bronze statue of a moose which stood at the entrance to the main street. Etched against the blue sky it was a truly magnificent sight.

Early the next morning, the car was difficult to start and the leaks in the radiator were getting worse. I decided to try to reach Winnipeg where I would have it completely overhauled. Crossing over to Manitoba, just west of Kenora, a thunderstorm blew up. Heavy black clouds hung low overhead and the road became so dark that I was forced to switch on my headlights. Driving rain slanted against the windscreen and purple streaks of lightning ripped the sky apart. It was frightening. Somehow the words of Newman's famous hymn came suddenly to my mind ......

> "Lead, kindly light, amid the encircling gloom,
> Lead thou me on!
> The night is dark and I am far from home ......"

I thought of the old Cornish miners who have sung this hymn all over the world, coming up in crowded cages from the bowels of the earth, their faces streaked with sweat and dirt, the deep burr of Cornwall still in their voices, ringing through the mines of South Africa, Australia and America. My reverie was interrupted as the storm ceased as abruptly as it had begun. As it grew lighter I saw with relief the outskirts of Winnipeg on the horizon. By the time I had reached the city, steam was hissing from the radiator and I realised, too late, that I was caught up in the rush hour traffic. I drove on along the main street, unable to escape. Through a haze of hot steam I could see the other drivers grinning as they drove past in their Buicks and Thunderbirds. One wag wound down his window and shouted, "I think your kettle is boiling ma'am!" At the first garage I saw, I sneaked out of line and tried to hide behind the petrol pumps. The mechanic told me there was a large hole in the radiator and that the universal joint would not last another mile. He said he could fix the radiator and put in a new joint, adding that if I thought I could get to Alaska in a car like that, I must be absolutely mad. I agreed with him, telling him that I would have missed a lot of thrills without a touch of insanity!

With the car repaired, next morning I headed west towards the Prairies. The change of scenery was dramatic. Among the pine forests I had seen but a little of the sky but now, the flat, desolate, empty land stretched ahead of me to the far horizon. There was no apparent sign of life, even the cattle grazing in the distance looked like statues and tall grain elevators stood stark and ghostly on the skyline. I switched on the car radio but no sound came from it. The stations were too far away to pick up a signal. I had an overwhelming sense of isolation, it was as if I had no identity. For five days I had scarcely spoken to anyone, except to ask for food or accommodation. There, in the middle of this vast, bleak, bitter land, the soft, green fields of Cornwall seemed part of another world.

After an overnight stop at Brandon I crossed the border into Saskatchewan, which is the name given to the River by the Cree Indians and means 'swift flowing.' Here, I put my watch back another hour from Central to Mountain Time. The car was going quite well and hopes of reaching Alaska were getting brighter. I drove carefully, keeping my speed down to fifty miles an hour as a rattle developed if I went any faster. Passing through Regina and Moose Jaw, I drove on across the flat, interminable prairies to Swift Current where I found the town preparing to celebrate Dominion Day on the first of July. Everywhere there was a hum of activity. Huge trucks lumbered through the streets, bringing in the bucking broncos, wild cattle and eager cowboys. Colourful flags fluttered from the buildings, so, caught up in the excitement, I decided to stay for two nights and spend the whole of the next day at the rodeo. The posters were advertising an unusual event which I wanted to see – a Chuckwaggon Race for small ponies. It was run on the same lines as its famous counterpart at Calgary but these were tiny, shaggy ponies, not much bigger than Shetlands. Harnessed to miniature chariots, they raced round at incredible speeds, their short little legs pounding on the ground like pistons and their long manes and tails flying wildly in the wind.

The next day I started on the last lap to Calgary where I had been invited to stay with a family called Schafer, whom I had never met but to whom I had been introduced by letter. Mrs. Schafer had been born in Cornwall and still kept in touch with Cornish friends, one of whom was Duncan Simpson, of the old established firm of Simpson Bros., the Penzance outfitters. It is to Duncan that I owe, not only the introduction to a wonderfully hospitable family but also the fact that I was invited to the legendary Calgary Stampede.

From Swift Current to Calgary it was a long drive of over three hundred miles. The sun beating down on the roof of the car turned the interior into a furnace. The steering wheel became almost too hot to touch after I had stopped for lunch. Just before I reached Medicine Hat, a gale blew up and I saw my first whirlwind. It spiralled into the air into a thick cloud of brown dust and disappeared. As the wind died down it became hotter and more humid and the engine began to overheat. The Schafers lived about four miles from Calgary and they had described a landmark for me. It was a tall hydro tower from which I could take my bearings to find my way to their home. I was only a mile from the house when suddenly I saw it, standing up like a fat sentry on the horizon. The car, however, as if sensing my smug satisfaction, was determined to have the last word! It began to cough and splutter and a jet of steam shot up from the radiator. I crawled on, steam whirling and eddying around the windscreen until I was forced to put my head out of the window to see the road ahead. Arriving in front of the Schafer house, I found Jill and Ed waiting for me with such a look of astonishment on their faces that we all dissolved into fits of laughter, even before introductions could be made. This mood of hilarity was the start of a most enjoyable week, engulfed in the friendly hospitality of the family. Jill and Ed were breeders of Yellow Labradors but their daughter, Sue, was more interested in horses, so the next day we all set off for Calgary to watch the world famous Stampede.

The Calgary Stampede has been held annually since 1886 but it wasn't until 1912 that the Stampede – the actual cowboy contests – became a feature. Since then, the festival has been known as the 'Calgary Exhibition and Stampede.' It lasts for nine days and during that time the town of Calgary throws its hat into the air and relives the colour and ceremony of the old ranching days. Gone is the sober, industrial town. A stranger walking through the streets on Stampede morning would be convinced that Time had suddenly gone in reverse and that he was back in the old pioneering days of the Wild West. Although we arrived early in the morning, people were already dancing in the streets; young and old alike were responding to the rhythm of the old prairie tunes and clapping to the beat of the Square Dance bands.

The girls were dressed in brightly coloured squaw dresses and the men wore cowboy rig. We ate pancakes and flapjacks which were being distributed free, steaming hot from the chuckwaggon stove and running with delicious butter and maple syrup. In the shops the assistants wore gaudy shirts, cowboy belts, broad-rimmed Stetsons and greeted us with a smile. Restaurants were advertising 'Round-up Breakfasts,' 'Chuckwaggon Lunches' and Buffalo Stew for the 'Cowhand Supper.' Everyone joined in the spirit of the occasion. From every rooftop flags fluttered in a dazzling array of colour under the hot sun.

At 9 a.m. the Stampede began. The main street was closed to traffic and thousands of people lined the sidewalks, sat on cushions in the road, perched on walls, while some of the bolder children climbed the lampposts and hung precariously from the tops. All the windows overlooking the street were crammed with eager faces, keen to watch the history of Canadian life being paraded before them. Every facet of Canadian life through the ages was represented, from the old carts drawn by buffalo and oxen right up to the most modern floats. The Royal Canadian Mounted Police led the massed bands, followed by representatives of the various Youth Clubs and Horse Associations. Then came the Indian tribes with their feathered head dresses, riding bareback and using rope bridles. For more than an hour we sat enthralled by this wonderful display, then we hurried over to the Stampede Grounds where the cowboys were flexing their muscles and waiting for their part in the pageantry to begin. To them, this was a serious business. The glamour rapidly fades when one is sitting on top of a wildly twisting, snorting bronco whose one aim is to ram one's face into the sun-baked earth. These are the professionals – tough, courageous men who follow the rodeo circuit. They make their living in a world of heat, dust and sweating horse flesh. In the few seconds it takes to stay aboard a bucking horse or a long-horned Brahma Bull a man can earn as much as ten thousand dollars. A versatile cowboy can take his pick of the contests – the saddle bronc, bareback riding, calf roping, steer wrestling, or bull riding, where the cash prizes run into thousands of dollars. At the end of the season the champions are very rich men. Boys of ten often start their rodeo careers by entering the Boys' Wild Steer Riding Contests. The young steers are carefully selected and graded according to size and weight for these contests.

One of the toughest events was the Wild Horse Race. In this, all the chutes were flung open at the same time and 16 raw, untamed horses were catapulted into the arena. None of them had ever been touched by man before being rounded up in the wilds of the Yukon or British Columbia. The contestants work in teams of three. Each team has already drawn for chute numbers and must catch the horse coming out of that particular chute by grabbing the long rope which trails from each head collar. One man stays at the end of the rope as an anchor, another attempts to hold the horse quiet, and the third tries to throw a saddle on him, mount and ride to the end of the arena. To the spectators it's a mad mêlée of galloping horses, swearing cowboys being dragged off their feet, saddles flying through the air and horses' hooves kicking up the dust as they fight for their freedom.

Of course, the spectacle that attracts the crowds, and the event that people come from all over the world to see, is the famous Chuckwaggon Race or Rangeland Derby. It originated in the pioneering days when cowboys used to harness up their horses and race each other into town after the day's work was done. A Hollywood producer once said, "These Chuckwaggon Races make the old Roman Chariot Races look like a Donkey Derby." It was certainly the wildest horse race I have ever seen. Each team consisted of four lean, hard-mouthed thoroughbreds, driven by a yelling cowboy and accompanied by four outriders. Although wild and dangerous, the race is governed by a strict code of rules. Penalties are imposed for infringements. At the starting signal, the outriders, who at this stage are unmounted, have to throw a stove, tent poles and canvas into the back of the wagon, then they mount their horses and accompany the rocking, tottering wagons which do a figure of eight around two barrels before they hit the race track for the half mile gallop to the finishing line. The wagons tilt at alarming angles and on several occasions have overturned and killed both men and horses, not surprisingly earning the nickname of 'Suicide Race.' The roar of the crowd, yells of the drivers and the pounding of hooves on the dirt track all combine to make it one of the most thrilling races in the world.

At the end of an exciting week it was time to move on again, but meanwhile I had received some depressing news. The mechanic who had mended the radiator of the car told me that the transmission was faulty and its chances of surviving the hazards of the Alaskan Highway were practically nil. He himself had driven on it and he explained that if a car breaks down, it costs about a hundred dollars to have it towed to the nearest garage, which could easily be a hundred miles away. It was tempting to take the risk as I was reluctant to give up after driving all those miles but the car had already cost me a lot of money in repairs and if it did break down I would not be able to afford the towing fee. Sadly, for I felt as if I were abandoning an old friend, I took the car into Calgary to a Ford garage. Much to my surprise I was told it was against the law to sell an American car in Canada, unless I paid an exorbitant import tax. This was a problem I hadn't envisaged. After discussing it with various customs and excise men, they convinced me that my only alternative, if I wanted to recoup the money I had spent on it, was to drive back over the border into the States and try to sell it there. It would have been foolhardy not to take their advice but the temptation to risk everything and drive on to Alaska was very strong. However, I decided discretion was the better part of valour and after studying a map, found that the nearest American town was Shelby, just over the border, in Montana – and two hundred miles south of Calgary.

Once again I was saying goodbye to friends whose kindness had made me feel so welcome. How many times since I left Cornwall had I said, 'hello and goodbye' I wondered. I had seen the interiors of many homes, breathed their atmosphere, become involved with the lives of the people who lived in them, then moved on. Some have become life-long friends, others ethereal figures of the past.

The drive to Shelby was very different from my drive across Canada. It had ceased to be an adventure, for I drove with a nagging sense of defeat. Was I being faint-hearted, or sensible in not risking the car on the notorious Alcan? Perhaps it wouldn't have broken down, then what elation I would have felt had I been able to make my 'triumphal entry' into Anchorage! The thought almost persuaded me to turn round again but the garage mechanic's warning was still fresh in my mind

'You've been very lucky to have got this far but I wouldn't give much for your chances in the mountains."

Luckily there were no mountains on the journey to Shelby. The country was flat and monotonous, similar to the wheat belt of the Prairies, even so, I was relieved to arrive safely. The task of disposing of the car was as difficult as I had expected but eventually I found a garage with an owner who had a sense of humour. At first he just laughed at the idea of buying such a car but after I had chatted him up for a while, he not only bought it but took me out to dinner to celebrate the deal! Without the car I felt strangely bereft. In a silly sort of way it had been a refuge and a convenient receptacle for all the bits and pieces collect on the long journey. I felt quite a pang of regret when I saw it being driven away.

Unfortunately there was no airport at Shelby, the nearest being eighty miles away at Great Falls, the birthplace of the American painter Charles Russell, who was well known for his portrayal of Western life. The next day I managed to get a lift into the town and in the early hours of the following morning caught a plane en route to Anchorage.

Alaska 1968

Chapter 13: **Alaska at last**

After a scheduled stop at Seattle, where there was a long delay owing to engine trouble, we eventually flew over Alaska at dawn. The sun-rise was turning the clouds into a delicate shade of candy floss pink and as we descended through them, the Alaskan countryside began to emerge. I suppose that like most people, I had always associated Alaska with snow and Eskimos, igloos and husky dogs but on this warm July morning as we flew towards Anchorage, I could see no evidence of any of them, except that the snow lingered on the peaks of the highest mountains. I could see no evidence either of any human habitation. The country was wild, rugged and breathtakingly beautiful. The water in the lakes was as clear as polished crystal and as we lost height, I could see the glowing colour of the fireweed, a dull red flower that grew in profusion and indeed made the mountains look as if they were on fire. There were patches too, of pale blue forget-me-nots, like handfuls of sky that had fallen at the water's edge. In spite of the magnificence of the scenery, I was overawed by the remoteness of this vast country and listened anxiously to the steady drone of the plane's engines. If we were forced to crash-land here, I had the feeling we would never be found. However, all was well, and like a mountain eagle coming gently to rest, we landed safely on the runway at Anchorage.

On the plane I had sat next to a young man who had come to Alaska to work on a building site and he offered to drive me to the Diamond H Ranch. According to the map it was about ten miles from the town, just off O'Malley Road, at the foot of the Chugach Mountains. Driving through Anchorage I was a little disappointed to find there was nothing to distinguish it from any other American town. I had half expected to see dog sleds in the main street and Eskimos in their heavy parkas but the only evidence of the latter was the souvenir shops which sell their hand-made crafts.

As we drove away from the town I could see the grape-blue mountains in the distance, looking even taller and more majestic than they had from the air. In a very short time we had left the traffic behind and were soon driving along a quiet

Diamond H Ranch
Alaska 1968

country road which seemed to be leading us into the wilderness. It meandered through forests of tall, slender pine trees, past crystal-clear lakes glowing pink in the reflection of the flaming fireweed. Suddenly a big bull moose lumbered out of the trees, right in front of the car. For a second all I could see was a huge pair of antlers blocking the windscreen but with amazing agility for such a large animal, he leapt for cover and vanished. On seeing him, I couldn't help feeling we were intruding on his territory. This wild and beautiful land belonged to the animals, to the trees and lakes, mountains and sky, not to man with his brash civilisation.

Just as I thought the road was leading us straight into the side of a mountain, it began to open out into a clearing and there ahead, was a black and white signboard which read,

'DIAMOND H RANCH – RIDING SCHOOL – BOARDING STABLES.'

Beside the road stood an attractive ranch-type house and behind it was a large, covered school, built directly on to the dwelling house itself. A few yards away was a white-fenced riding ring in which some riders were exercising their horses. As I thanked the young man for driving me to the ranch, a tall, dark woman came out of the house and greeted me with a smile. "I'm Mrs. Taplin – come and meet my husband and my daughter Linda." I walked into a spacious living-room in which an enormous window looked directly into the indoor school. Mr. Taplin and his teenage daughter were watching a client putting a horse through his paces. They both bid me a friendly welcome and with typical American cordiality we were soon chatting easily as the Taplins explained how the school had started.

Howard Taplin, an ex-cavalry officer, was one of the first men to drive a truckload of horses up the Alaskan Highway from 'outside' – the term used by Alaskans for the territory beyond Alaska. It took him five days to overcome the hazards of the Highway's choking dust, potholes and the sharp bends of the narrow, twisting road that someone once compared with the 'wild ramblings of a drunken moose.' In summer there is so much dust stirred up by the traffic that motorists are obliged to use their headlights throughout the day and in winter the frozen snow makes driving a dangerous adventure. With his handful of horses, Mr. Taplin taught a few children to ride. His lessons became so popular that he gradually worked up a thriving business and was able to build on more stabling and also take horses at livery. Boxes for 50 horses were built on to the covered school, which meant that in winter, when the temperature sometimes drops as low as thirty degrees below zero, the horses could be taken into the ring without having to venture outside. The indoor school was well lit by electricity, a necessity in an Alaskan winter, where it gets dark at three o'clock in the afternoon and stays so until ten o' clock the next morning.

Mr. Taplin explained some of the problems and difficulties that arise from running a school in a place as remote as Alaska, where all supplies have to be flown in, brought by ship from Seattle or Prince Rupert, or trucked along the Alcan. Prior to the last war there was no land route into Alaska. Planners had said it was an impossible task and that the cost would be prohibitive. Then came Pearl Harbour and the possibility of a blockade of the North Pacific ports. It was quickly decided that a road had to be put through. Incredibly, in only eight months, teams of American and Canadian engineers hacked their way through forests, swamps and mountains to complete the road which has now become known all over the world as 'The Alcan.'

At the outset it was understood that my job at the Diamond H was to be temporary and for the first week I wondered when I was going to be asked to do any work. The Taplin's hospitality was such that I was included in all their social activities. We went to the local horse show, visited friends and on several occasions I was taken to see the Cowboy Polo matches, a modified version of the conventional game which the horsemen of the district played for fun at the weekends. I think the most memorable of my experiences in Alaska, though, were the solitary rides on the mountain trails. Quite often I was asked to exercise some of the clients' horses and I would ride for miles, climbing higher and higher, the sun warm on my back and the reins loose on the horse's neck, letting him pick his own way along the narrow, rocky paths. In the cloister-like silence, the only sound was the creak of leather and the occasional click of the horse's shoe against a rock. Sometimes I would catch a glimpse of a moose as it disappeared into the trees, or the horse would be startled by a covey of Ptarmigans – little Alaskan game birds – who would suddenly scatter right under his nose. Once, I thought I caught sight of a brown bear but it vanished so quickly, I was not sure. I loved those quiet rides and whenever I was obliged to take parties of clients with me, I didn't enjoy the ride. Their incessant chatter seemed to me an affront to this peaceful land where I felt it was more natural to whisper than talk aloud.

Most of the riding taught at the Diamond H was Western but I found a growing interest in what the pupils called 'The English Hunting Seat.' They were keen to learn about English horse shows and I noticed that the word 'dressage' always cropped up whenever riding in England was discussed. I began giving a few private lessons and to earn some extra money I also taught at the nearby American Air Force base at Elmendorf, where they ran their own riding school. There are, understandably, only three riding schools in the whole of Alaska, the Diamond H, the one at Elmendorf and another at Fairbanks but interest and enthusiasm for horses are rapidly increasing. The Alaskans have a saying, 'Show me a land where there aint no horses and I'll show you a land where there aint no men.' The pioneering spirit of the old ranching days is still there in the present generation. Homesteads, horse barns and riding rings are literally hewn out of the countryside. Perhaps it is their spectacular mountains which are said to 'exalt the strong and daunt the weak' which are an inspiration to the Alaskan horse people, for they work tremendously hard to keep their horses, despite their isolated geographical position and the ever-escalating costs.

Most of the clients at the school lived reasonably near but one day some Missionaries brought a party of Eskimo children from one of the remote settlements to see the horses. Those dark-eyed, brown-faced youngsters had never ridden a horse in their lives, in fact, they had probably never even seen a live one. Their excited faces were a study in what I can only describe as 'fearful joy.' They were shy, rather timid children but their impeccable manners put some of our more sophisticated youth to shame.

At the Diamond H there was a variety of horses at livery; thoroughbreds, Quarter Horses, Tennessee Walking Horses and American Saddlebreds, - each requiring to be ridden in a slightly different manner. I shall never forget my first experience of riding a Five Gaited Saddlebred. It was a big, black gelding of about 17 hands, called Prince. He was a magnificent looking horse but I had no idea of how to get him to perform the rack, which is the fifth gait. Suddenly, however, something startled him and I found myself being carried round the arena at an incredible speed. It wasn't a gallop, nor was it a trot but his feet were moving in a distinct four-beat rhythm at a pace which was so smooth that I could have drunk a cup of tea while riding him without spilling any.

In the few weeks that I had been at the ranch I came to know some of the clients very well and with typical American friendliness they suggested that I stayed on to teach them more about English riding. It was, however, the beginning of September and I was obliged to leave before the winter set in.

It was the accepted custom in Alaska that if anyone required a lift down the Alcan, an advertisement would be put in the local newspaper. Usually you offered to share the petrol expenses or help with the driving in return for a lift 'outside!' I thought this was an excellent idea. Among the replies from the advert which I placed in the Anchorage Times, was one from a family consisting of mother, daughter and son who happened to be driving all the way to Cleveland. As I had left most of my luggage there, it seemed to be an ideal opportunity to be driven right to my destination. In due course we arranged to meet on the day before they were due to leave. The mother looked pale and haggard and her offspring, who were both in their early twenties, snapped bad temperedly at each other even while we were introducing ourselves. Their attitude spoiled my anticipation of the trip but I thought I would be able to keep out of their domestic squabbles and enjoy the scenery. How wrong I was!

We left Anchorage late in the afternoon of the following day, after a delay of two hours as the son had forgotten to check the spare wheel and had found it punctured. There was also a heated argument as to who should drive. They hurled abuse at one another until, no doubt worn out by their tirade, they all lapsed into a sulky silence. The boy took the wheel and began to drive like a maniac. The first part of the Alcan out of Anchorage is a good, paved road and the speedometer hovered between 90 and 95 miles an hour. Instead of looking at the countryside, I was unable to tear my eyes away from the oncoming traffic and when it grew dark, the headlights flashed past in a dazzling blur. At our first stop for petrol I suggested that I might drive but the daughter decided to take over. Her driving was even more erratic than her brother's. At last we came to the unpaved section of the highway and I thought that at least we would slow down but they drove over potholes and round hairpin bends with complete disregard for safety. My hopes of enjoying the scenery faded rapidly in a cloud of choking brown dust. At one stage a headlamp was smashed by a flying stone and I was thankful for a brief respite while it was being mended. On asking why they were in such a hurry I was informed, curtly, that an appointment in Cleveland made it imperative that they arrive within five days. They planned to drive day and night, taking it in turns to sleep. I soon became convinced we would all be killed long before reaching Cleveland! I was much too frightened to sleep and when the nightmare journey ended eventually, I staggered out of the car, so exhausted that my mind had almost ceased to function. It was a weird feeling of complete disorientation. Unable to face the thought of talking to anyone, I booked into a motel and slept for twelve hours.

The next morning, refreshed and ready to face the world again, I spent a few days with my Cleveland friends before flying to Bermuda, where I had arranged to stay with some relatives before returning home.

So, for me, another journey had ended and another chapter of my life had been written. Horses have been my passport to a varied and interesting life. It is through them that I have made many friends, some of whom I may never see again but I shall always be grateful to them for smoothing my path and giving me a helping hand along the way.

What happened next...

In 1973 Ann married John Brock and went to live in the little Cornish fishing village of Coverack.

Her love of travel continued, and together they visited Europe, Russia and South Africa. To her delight, John was invited to lecture on Cornish Mining in Grass Valley, California and Nevada U.S.A. entailing yet another fascinating visit to America.

In 1976 John was awarded the O.B.E. for his services to Cornwall.

John died in September, 2000 and Ann still lives in the same coastguard cottage overlooking the sea at Coverack.

Goldflake's granddaughter
MANACLE MIST
performing some of her tricks

Doing the Spanish Walk
in Coverack 1984

Going shopping

Returning home with groceries

**Ann and Manacle Mist
smile for the camera**

Crossing her legs on command
Please don't try this at home!!

Taking a bow